Praying with Jesus

Also by Rob Warner

Alive in the Spirit
Prepare for Revival
Walking with God

PRAYING WITH JESUS

Experiencing the spiritual riches of the Lord's Prayer

ROB WARNER

Hodder & Stoughton
LONDON SYDNEY AUCKLAND

First published in Great Britain in 1999

10 9 8 7 6 5 4 3 2 1

British Library Cataloguing in Publication Data
A record for this book is available from the British Library

ISBN 0 340 72182 0

Typeset by Avon Dataset Ltd, Bidford-on-Avon, Warks

Printed and bound in Great Britain by
Clays Ltd, St Ives plc

Hodder and Stoughton Ltd
A Division of Hodder Headline PLC
338 Euston Road
London NW1 3BH

This book is dedicated to the churches where I have had the privilege to serve, whose members and leaders have taught me so much about the gospel of Jesus Christ:

Buckhurst Hill Baptist,
Herne Hill Baptist,
QRC,
and our new church in Wimbledon,
that is launching even as I write.

Contents

Introduction

As a young child I was introduced to the Lord's Prayer by means of a full-colour gift book. Each left-hand page provided the next phrase of Jesus' prayer in the resounding cadences of the Authorised Version, while each right-hand page illustrated the text with a full-page, full-colour picture in a style suitable for the under fives. Night by night my parents took me through the book, teaching me the words and introducing me to the experience of prayer. I was given the book before I learned to read, and so I memorised the words by repetition, saying aloud the words to be found on each page when the actual writing was still entirely unintelligible – a common talent in the very young that unfailingly impresses unsuspecting adults. At that tender age my parents bestowed upon me gifts that would last a lifetime: a love of books, the gift of praying, and a fascination and admiration for Jesus, who remains the most towering influence any civilisation has ever known.

The prayer that a young child prayed nightly is with me still. Whether we want to begin to learn to pray or to go deeper in prayer, there is no greater resource than this. In its simplicity, it is a truly universal prayer, capable of being understood by the youngest. In its profundity, it is a prayer of inexhaustible depths. In its sparse poetry, it is a prayer of great beauty, without a single word or phrase that is superficial or surplus to requirements. The prayer of the Master is the unsurpassable prayer of prayers, the Everest of Christian spirituality. The Psalms of David are searching evocations of the heights and depths of human experience, but the Lord's Prayer stands alone. It is the prayer for all times and every person. From the towering heights of Manhattan to the mud huts of a primitive tribe, from the youngest children with the power of speech to octogenarian great-grandparents on their death bed, the timeless words of Jesus express more richly than any others the longings, hopes and fears of men and women before the living God. My prayer for this book is twofold:

> that believers might break free
>   from the headlong rush of modern living
> and recapture an experience of daily existence
>   shot through with intimations of eternity
>
> and that those who have never discovered personal faith
>   in our hectic and secularised world
> might pause for a moment and consider anew
>   the hidden depths to human existence
> that can never find adequate expression or fulfilment
>   upon the treadmill of consumerism.

There is indeed something more, a spirituality to recover and explore, and there is no finer place to begin than the prayer that Jesus bequeathed to the world.

As with my previous exploration of spirituality, *Walking with God*, the chapters are subdivided into short sections in order to make the book useful in a variety of ways. *Praying with Jesus* will lend itself to being read straight through like any other book, to being studied chapter by chapter in a home group, or to being used in short sections as an inspiration for daily prayer. In *Walking with God*, each chapter was introduced by a hymn from William Cowper and ended with one from Charles Wesley. This time I have chosen to begin each chapter with a poem by George Herbert. There is an elegant simplicity in his explorations of living faith, together with a rewarding honesty about times of spiritual dryness. The concluding poet is John Donne. While he was writing his divine sonnets, Donne's faith was tempestuous, even tortured. There is a passionate and lyrical intensity to Donne's poetry that evokes perhaps better than any other English writer what it means to wrestle with faith, doubt competing with hope, sin with obedience. The poetry of Donne and Herbert is quite different, which underlines the simple truth, so often forgotten, that living faith is by no means restricted to one personality type.

In the introduction to *Walking with God*, I said that I hoped to write a sequel that would explore the Lord's Prayer and the Lord's Supper. The first five chapters of *Praying with Jesus* focus upon the Lord's Prayer, and the sixth turns to the breaking of bread. There is a risk in considering this latter, glorious theme that denominational differences might provoke unwanted controversy. That is certainly not my intention. My prayer, on the contrary, is that readers will find much benefit in the reflections on the meal of Jesus, irrespective of their particular denomination or stream.

Each chapter also includes a selection of devotional poetry, which I hope many will find rewarding and stimulating for their own life of prayer. Whereas in *Walking with God* I provided a selection of prayers and poems in which most writers were only represented once, in *Praying with Jesus* I have chosen to concentrate on a more restricted number of Christian poets, including Ben Jonson, Sir Walter Ralegh, Gerard Manley Hopkins and William Cowper, as well as Donne and Herbert. This allows the reader to see these major Christian poets explore a wide range of different moods and conditions of personal and practical Christian spirituality.

I would never be able to write without the constant support and encouragement of my dear wife, Claire, to whom I am ever grateful.

My sons, James and Tom, have also played their part in helping me complete this book. My thanks also to Debbie Haine, my super-efficient PA, and to Annabel Robson, my ever-patient editor at Hodders.

Rob Warner
Trinity Sunday 1998

CHAPTER I

OUR FATHER IN HEAVEN, HALLOWED BE YOUR NAME

Our Father, who art in heaven,
hallowed be thy Name

PRAYER

Prayer the Church's banquet, angels' age,
God's breath in man returning to his birth,
The soul in paraphrase, heart in pilgrimage,
The Christian plummet sounding heav'n and earth;
Engine against th'Almighty, sinners' tower,
Reversed thunder, Christ-side-piercing spear,
The six-days' world transposing in an hour,
A kind of tune, which all things hear and fear;
Softness, and peace, and joy, and love, and bliss,
Exalted manna, gladness of the best,
Heaven in ordinary, man well dressed,
The milky way, the bird of Paradise,
Church-bells beyond the stars heard, the soul's blood,
The land of spices; something understood.

George Herbert, 1593–1633

1

Our Father

Relationships have never been so brittle. Families are fragmented as young adults move far away in search of qualifications, work or promotion. Few people keep in close touch with childhood friends. Many are unable to get beyond a nodding acquaintance with neighbours, not wishing to intrude or simply lacking the time to cultivate the traditional virtues of neighbourliness. More and more of our instinctive relational needs must be met within the confines of our own home and a small social circle. What was once provided within a stable, local community that established a settled context for the individual from cradle to grave must now for increasing numbers be fulfilled almost exclusively by the marriage relationship. Our partner has become our best friend, our lover, our family and the financial co-contributor to our self-contained micro-community. Small wonder that marriage itself is under threat: many relationships struggle to support the extra demands and expectations imposed upon an isolated couple in today's world.

We are pinioned at the turn of the millennium between two contradictory impulses. The instinctive need to belong makes us yearn for the security of a stable network of lasting relationships. But the fragmentariness of post-modern living means that we inhabit a world in which the time we need to nurture relationships has been stripped from the schedule of life priorities. In June 1998 a British public opinion poll revealed that many parents regretfully confess to missing out on key moments of their children's development because of the pressures of work. Growing numbers of women experience an inner tension between the desire to pursue a successful career and the relentless ticking of the biological clock that sets a limit upon their child-bearing years.

Morality is considered private and personal – 'Don't you try to tell me what to do!' Spirituality is similarly private, treated as an optional extra, or even patronised as an obsolete indulgence for the emotionally inadequate. Behind the net curtains of suburbia and in tenement tower blocks, millions live isolated and shallow lives. No doubt life in the old rural communities was often constricting and narrowly conformist. We have entered an age of new liberty to discover our true selves and shape our own destinies. Our path through life is no longer rigidly predetermined, for women by their gender and for men by their father's wealth or trade. Good though it is to be liberated from the iron grip of societal determinism, the pendulum has swung so far that now we experience the blight of hyper-individualism, an excessive isolation in which increasing numbers have little sense of belonging and no longer have any place they can really call home. We have become the rootless generation, a nomadic age of migrant workers.

For an atomised society in which community is becoming an endangered experience, the prayer of Jesus begins with startling force. His opening phrase immediately reveals that living prayer needs to find corporate and not just individual expression, for his prayer begins in the first person plural: *OUR* Father. This is not a way of praying that can find full expression in splendid isolation. Jesus takes us to the heart of what it means to be human, for we have been created as relational beings. Thus the callous power of solitary confinement – our full humanity cannot find expression stripped of the opportunity to commune with others. We find ourselves not in the absence of others but in the enriching stimuli, the pleasure and pain, of friendship and intimacy.

To pray to *our* Father is to recognise at once the two dimensions of relationships that give depths of meaning and vitality to our lives. We are made for relationship with God and we are made for relationship with one another. Jesus celebrated the pivotal importance of relationships to human identity and fulfilment when asked to summarise the Jewish law (Matt. 22:35–40). Looking beyond the ritual requirements of the Temple religion and the Ten Commandments' necessary restrictions on negative and destructive behaviour, Jesus emphasised the primacy of loving relationships: to love God with the entirety of our being, and to love our neighbours as we love ourselves.

This relational pivot to human existence finds its origin in the nature of the triune God. Some shrink from any talk of the Trinity. Here is such mystery, such subtle complexity, that they hardly dare to speak about such things. Others are quickly perplexed by the algebraic befuddlement of three in one and one in three, perhaps secretly wondering whether the Trinity is a convoluted, tortuous and unnecessarily elaborate concept, concocted by academic theologians to wile away long, winter evenings by the fireside of a medieval university. Nothing could be further from the truth. To be sure, as Augustine warned, if anyone thinks they have fully understood the Trinity they have not even begun to understand. Nonetheless, this doctrine arises not from speculation but from experience. Jesus related to God the Father as a distinct person, and invited his followers to enter into a similar way of relating to the unseen Lord of hosts – as the heavenly Father, God gives himself to us. However, the first believers could only make sense of their eyewitness encounters with Jesus by confessing that he was nothing less than the Son of God, come in human flesh: in Christ God gives himself to us a second time. And then, at the day of Pentecost, even as Jesus had promised, in another distinctive way, the same God gave himself to Jesus' followers a third time. Out of this experience of three modes of visitation by the same God developed the understanding that, within the Godhead, Father, Son and Holy Spirit have been eternally co-existent, communing together in perfect relationships of love, since before the dawn of time. In three distinct persons there is absolute oneness. Undivided and undiminished love is the essential being of God, as John affirmed when summing up the essence of Christian doctrine: 'God is love' (1 John 4:16).

We have been fashioned in the image of the triune God, not as isolated individuals, but as men and women together. To be made in the image of the triune God is to be created for relationship, with God and also with one another. While some religions segregate men from women and give them distinctive prayers, as if access to deeper spirituality was determined by gender, Jesus gives one prayer for all. Men and women, Jews and Gentiles, everyone is included in the same prayer. As we make the united declaration, '*Our Father*', the dividing walls of sexism and racism, snobbery and, yes, even denominationalism, are reduced to rubble.

True religion, according to Jesus, is not some private affair, between me and God alone. His prayer begins by acknowledging, indeed affirming and enjoying, our commonality. We have a shared humanity, born for relationships, and as we pray together we affirm not only a common faith, but a common source of existence. In every repetition of this one word, *our*, the community of faith is reborn. Whenever we pray in this way together, we are invited to delight in all that we share. Whatever our differences of background or qualifications, abilities or income, gender, generation or race, in the opening phrase of the Lord's Prayer we acknowledge and choose to accept one another. As we truly pray these words, they anchor us to one another. We express inclusivity. We affirm not only that we belong to God, but also that we belong together.

Our Father

Personal reflection

What small, practical effort could you make to include someone who tends to be marginalised, at your church or workplace?

2

Heavenly Father

When a BBC news reader suggested a few years ago that news programmes should contain more positive stories, he was widely pilloried by his journalistic peers. Although the public might enjoy upbeat and sentimental features, the staple diet of journalism has always been crises, conflicts and disasters. It is decidedly difficult, almost impossible, for something that is good and uncontroversial to become in any sense newsworthy. Life in the developed world may no longer be nasty, brutish and short, but its shadow side remains inescapable. Sooner or later, every family will skirmish with suffering, whether miscarriages or cancer, unemployment or marriage breakdown, dementia or premature death. In every waking moment, someone somewhere is blissfully happy while someone else is racked with agony, writhing on a death bed of pain. For every nation that celebrates peace and democracy and enjoys a steady rise in gross domestic product, others struggle with warfare and civil strife, totalitarian regimes and remorselessly rising interest payments on international loans. The news headlines demonstrate an ineluctable reality: like a coal seam running through the earth, there is a vein of suffering that runs continually through human existence.

Life is complex and ambiguous. Robert Browning's poem 'Pippa passes' celebrated the essentially positive nature of life: 'God's in his heaven, all's right with the world.' However, other poets have been more aware of life's joys tarnished by the bleakness of suffering and so they more readily trace the rain than the rainbow. Thomas Hardy, that great novelist and prophet of doubt and disbelief, suggested that the twentieth century might be characterised by generations who would feel increasingly ensnared by the empty sorrows of a godless and meaningless existence.

Some turn to religion for escape, for a way to deny or avoid the harsher side of life. From time to time new religious movements arise claiming that all suffering is illusory or entirely avoidable, if only the right mental attitudes are cultivated. Such notions are remote from real Christianity. We follow a crucified Saviour. Yes, he was raised from the dead, triumphing over mortality. But first he had to endure a vicious flogging and beating and then suffer a protracted and painful death. The life-force drained slowly from him with the emptying of his veins as he fought for breath, bearing down upon the nails that pinioned him in his struggle to fill his lungs with one more gasp of air. The religion of Jesus offers no instant access to a pain-free existence. He offers no false hope of an easy journey through life. His faith enabled him to walk the way of the cross, and his followers can discover a similar strength in the Holy Spirit: courage to endure and the prospect of coping with life not on our own, nor in our own resources, but with the presence and sustaining comfort of God.

Those with a sunny disposition may never find it difficult to think of God as Father, but such a statement is by no means self-evident. To suggest that God relates to us as Father is hardly an obvious conclusion, automatically and unambiguously drawn from everyone's experience of life. But Jesus puts God as Father centre stage. A few rabbis had taken the risk of suggesting that God can in some ways be compared to a Father, but only Jesus dared to go so far as to address God directly as Abba, without apology or qualification. His favourite term for referring to God – Abba, in the Aramaic language that he spoke – was so compelling to the first Christians, so pivotal to their own experience of God in their new-found faith, that they used Jesus' Aramaic word in their Greek-speaking churches (Rom. 8:15; Gal. 4:6).

Jesus is no shallow sentimentalist. He is certainly not offering a spirituality based upon the idea 'Wouldn't it be nice if God were like a dad?' Fully recognising the ambiguity of human existence, the rough inescapably entwined with the smooth, and taking full account of his own precarious existence once he had stirred up the hostility of the Jewish and Roman authorities, Jesus provides an emphatic affirmation of divine fatherliness. The notion of God as Father does not begin with human theorising, it begins in the heart of God. In the simple word, *Father*, Jesus gives us a promise with the power to endure. Notwithstanding those moments in personal or national history when the shadows seem ready to engulf every last glimmer of hope, the word of the Lord still stands. No matter how much our circumstances may promise only despair and the furtherance of sorrow, God has revealed himself to us as Father. In this second word of Jesus' great prayer we make a remarkable statement of faith. Irrespective of the news headlines or our personal circumstances or feelings, we embrace the promise of revelation: more than the most dedicated of good and caring earthly fathers, the heavenly Father encircles us with his love.

In one word Jesus provides his followers with a distinctive perspective on life in its totality, a new way of seeing. To make the opening declaration, 'Our Father', is to declare that we choose to look upon life from the vantage point of faith. The first given of life, deeper than its hopes and fears, joys and sorrows, is the fatherliness of the living God. Here is revelation and mystery: a declaration that gives us confidence in every circumstance of life, and yet a mystery that chastens the limits of human understanding. We can never unravel the mystery of suffering, and yet these two things we know: we have a God who has entered into suffering with us, embracing death for our sake at the cross; and this God who takes our suffering into his own existence reveals himself to us, deeper than every bewilderment we may ever know in the anguish and abandonment of dread pain and sorrow, as the Fatherly God, grounding our existence in his unshakable love.

This promise of divine fatherliness anchors our existence in the face of suffering and emphatically points us towards Jesus. He not only declares that God is Father, he puts flesh on the doctrine. When his followers asked him to show them the Father, his response was clear and emphatic: 'whoever has seen me has seen the Father' (John 14:9). The character of the Father is revealed in the Son. We begin to understand God as Father not by our own experiences of being fathered or fathers. Our grasp of God as Father must be grounded in the person of his Son: his words, his character, his life, death and resurrection. To pray to God the Father is therefore to declare a multiple dependence upon the Son: he brings us the revelatory word; he gives substance to the promise in his revelatory life; he mediates this new and living way of knowing God as Father through the atoning sacrifice of his death. The simple phrase, '*Our Father*', carries with it an implicit and necessary dependence upon Christ. It is only because of Jesus, his life, his teaching and his death for all humankind, that we can presume to approach the living God as Father.

Familiarity can make us oblivious to the bold faith of this first declaration of Jesus' prayer. We have lost the shock of the new. But in this opening phrase is a resounding affirmation of faith. When we pray to the Father and mean it, we look beyond the superficialities of our present experience, good or difficult, and take afresh into our mind and heart the revelatory words of Jesus. Just as some ancient instruments have a bass note that pulses regularly beneath the melody line, here is the bass note of the life of discipleship. Far beyond the highs and lows of personal experiences and feelings, with a depth and durability utterly different from the disposable transience of today's pop icons, fashion statements and news headlines, here is the constant ground swell, the basso profundo of human existence: God has given himself to us as our heavenly Father.

Prayer response

Pray for someone you know whose life is a struggle, that they may discover new hope in the fatherhood of God.

3

My Father

Some of the most important conversations need few words. A couple besottedly in love may devote entire conversations to no more than sighing out their loved one's name, gazing deeply into one another's eyes. At moments of personal tragedy or pressure, just to have someone say your name with tenderness can bring more comfort than a thousand well-intentioned words. For me, faced with the most beautiful scenery or human artistry or struggling with moments of acute personal strain, the most eloquent conversation, whether sharing joy or sorrow, providing or seeking strength and support, is simply to speak my wife's name – 'Oh Claire!'

In the playground of a nursery school, many children will cry out for the only person who can provide the medication of tender love for their grazed knee: 'I want my mummy!' Teachers and carers of the very young will also know times when a child, in a moment of pleasure or achievement, will suddenly call them 'mummy'! There is a tenderness in speaking the names of those to whom we are closest, a simplicity and directness in the most intimate of conversations. In the company of those we know less well, conversation is much more likely to swing between the extremes of awkward silence, where we feel we ought to say something but nothing comes to mind, or to a breathless torrent of voluble chatter, embarrassed by any threatening hint of silence.

To pray to God as 'Father' seems overwhelmingly incongruous. How can we presume to address the Lord of the cosmos, transcendent in majesty, awesome in power, in language that speaks of domestic intimacy? Such informality may seem irreverent, even presumptuous and impudent. We would make so much more of an effort to choose appropriate terms of respect if faced with a monarch or mayor, a prime minister or a president. And yet, of course, it is Jesus who has emphatically sanctioned this new way of praying. The living God, he insisted, will not stand on ceremony, and does not require the piling up of honorific epithets before he will turn an attentive ear to our requests.

When we pray to God as Father, we are not merely engaged in a superficial imitation of Jesus. We are making his way of praying our own. To pray 'our Father' is not only to acknowledge an underlying oneness with all who echo this prayer. It also and necessarily carries the meaning '*my* Father'. This radical way of praying demands a personal act of faith. Only when we embrace the invitation to respond to God as our personal, heavenly Father can we begin to enter into Jesus' way of praying.

A father is meant to be someone you can trust. Someone you can turn to in moments of need. A good father wants to cultivate in his children a sense of confidence and security. He becomes a safety net for their self-belief, not a brooding and fearful shadow in the background, a cold-hearted and over-demanding disciplinarian. A wise father seeks to nurture a relationship that is to be enjoyed, not endured.

To pray to God as Father is to declare an underlying security of relationship; a trust that means we will lean upon God with all our weight; an acknowledgment of Fatherly love at the fulcrum of human existence, beyond the enigmatic uncertainties, the underlying transience, of personal circumstances. It is a prayer not only of personal faith, but of intimacy. There is a quantum leap of faith between saying, 'I believe in the existence of God,' and praying to God as

Father. For many in the ancient world, the gods were positively dangerous. Worship was about placating powerful and capricious deities, who might at any moment play havoc with their human devotees, destroying their crops, switching allegiance to their enemies, or even, most notably in the case of Zeus, deceiving and raping women on a regular basis. Even today, world religions with a fierce and one-dimensional view of God as the righteous judge could not contemplate praying to God as Father. Such intimacy is inconceivable, in some cases even intolerable. But Jesus' prayer quietly affirms that the guiding principle of the cosmos is nothing less than a love that is both divine and fatherly, all-embracing and yet intimate.

There are times when the simple cry of 'Father' sums up all that needs to be said in prayer. I remember holding our first baby in my hands, within moments of his birth. Experiencing the miracle of the gift of life, the awesome responsibility and privilege of parenthood, to say 'Father' was a cry of amazement and delight. At times when I am travelling I will go walking in beautiful countryside alone, or visit an art gallery. When there is no human company with whom to share exquisite beauty, whether fashioned in creation or by an artist's hands, an appreciative cry of 'Father!' is enough to make sure the pleasure *is* shared.

Anyone involved in pastoral ministry will inevitably need to try to provide some kind of support for people whose circumstances are horrendous. It is wonderful to see someone healed from a debilitating illness, or a childless couple finally being able to conceive, but at other times we must comfort the dying and the bereaved, or sustain a couple whose experience of repeated miscarriages ends not with a live birth but with lifelong childlessness. In sorrow, disappointment and confusion as well as in moments of exultant joy, this prayer of one word, provided for us by Jesus, allows us to draw upon the Fatherly love that is the foundation of the cosmos. To pray to 'my heavenly Father' is certainly a prayer of personal faith, and speaks of the need for inner decision in response to Christ's teaching, rather than a merely outward and shallow conformity to institutional religion. But 'my Father' is far more than a prayer of conversion. It is a new perspective on life, a new way of seeing; a resolve to hold fast to Fatherly love, not only in the moments when life is bursting with enjoyment, fulfilment and pleasure, but even when divine goodwill is hidden, cast into the shadows by headlines of famine, tragedy and war or the personal hardships of a difficult season of life. Whether our experience is more like the apparent disaster of Good Friday, the empty, in-between time of Easter Saturday, or the triumph of Easter Sunday, still the same prayer can enrich our lives. In every kind of circumstance, we can determine to make this prayer our own: 'Father, *my* Father!'

Personal reflection

Is your faith personal, living and thriving, or is it becoming little more than a merely theoretical assent to the gospel?

4

In heaven

To declare that God is in his heaven is to assert that the cosmos is in the best of hands. We do not pray to one god among many who happens to be benign and fatherly, but who may have equally powerful rivals of less savoury demeanour. It is the one Lord of the cosmos, the Giver of Life and the Ruler over all existence, whom we approach as our Father in heaven.

Our prayers are therefore addressed to the One with supreme authority. This gives us double confidence. Our Father is the Sovereign Lord, and therefore our requests are far more than pious pleas, for he has the capacity to answer every petition. But this is no genie rubbed from a lamp, compelled to fulfil every demand, irrespective of its wisdom and foresight. Folk tales abound with foolish peasants wasting three wishes on trivial impulses:

'I wish I had a sausage!'

'What a waste of a wish. I wish that sausage was stuck on your nose!'

'We're as stupid as each other! I wish the sausage to be gone!'

The living God has the power to answer our requests, but he also has untrammelled authority. Ours is to submit our petitions, his to sift the wheat from the chaff, the wise and timely from the well-intentioned folly. No manner of praying, however eloquent or impassioned, no matter how many well-turned phrases or how high the decibels, can impose our petty desires and limited perspective upon the Lord of the universe. We submit requests for others because love demands that we must. We rejoice when our prayers are wonderfully fulfilled. But living faith is not dependent upon the success rate of our intercession. When our prayers seem to make no difference, whether for individuals or for nations in desperate need, still the Lord's Prayer insists upon the immovable truth of divine authority and wisdom: our Father is always in his heaven. We can therefore pray with confidence and humility. Confidence, because it is the sovereign Lord to whom we bring our petitions. Humility, because the ultimate authority is his, never ours.

To pray to our Father in heaven brings together two essential strands of a Christian understanding of God. As Father, God is immanent, present and available in his love. In heaven, God is transcendent, exalted beyond the capacity of the human mind to grasp, in the mystery of his infinite otherness. In one phrase Jesus combines these twin truths. When we lose sight of either aspect, our understanding of God is instantly distorted.

Immanence without transcendence leads to a misapplied mateyness, an irreverent and trivialising diminution of the exalted Lord of the cosmos. Granted the right to address God as Father, we presume to domesticate him, reduce his awesome infinitude to the modest scale of a household deity. Immanence alone leads to a God without the mystery of inaccessible depths of glory and power.

Transcendence without immanence leads to awe without intimacy. We may acknowledge fear and trembling before the divine, but such a God is remote from human concerns in his majestic otherness. There is no possibility of interpersonal intimacy, no I–you or child–Father dimension of encounter. Transcendence alone leads to a God beyond knowing.

When Elijah confronted the priests of Baal, he taunted them that their frenzied prayers were producing no results, no matter how intense their insistence, how fervent their self-mutilation. Perhaps they should shout louder, he chided with biting sarcasm, in case Baal was deep in thought, preoccupied with other demands, away on business or even sleeping (1 Kings 18:27). To pray to our Father in heaven is to address the one who provides unrestricted access, for there is no limit on his attentiveness or his willingness and power to act. God's heavenly dwelling place might suggest the possibility of remoteness, and an indifference to earthly concerns, like Nero indulging his notorious excesses at the imperial palace, while Rome was consumed by fire. But Jesus' incarnation within the dimensions of space and time assures us that God's nature is always to remain involved with his creation and available to those who pray.

Traditional Western notions of heaven have little to do with the Bible. For some it is a kind of half-life, a wispy and ethereal existence, a pale and insipid echo of life on earth. Others think of heaven in terms of being perched upon a cloud playing a harp. When I first came across such notions as a young teenager, I immediately feared that heaven sounded immensely dull, an interminable plucking of strings in an eternal music class. If that was the sum of heaven, I concluded, eternity was going to feel like a very long time indeed!

The most important New Testament clues to the nature of life in heaven are found in the visions of John and the resurrection appearances of Jesus. In the book of Revelation, there is a vivid and precise description of heaven as the new Jerusalem (Rev. 21). Heaven is a city, which speaks not of pollution, traffic congestion and crime, but of a relational community, far removed from the tedious isolation of single-occupancy clouds. The city walls are constructed from many kinds of precious stone. John's list of which stones are used at each level of the walls is bewildering to those who don't know one precious stone from another. The real point, of course, is not literal but suggestive. John's concern is not to enable us to construct a scale model of the new Jerusalem, but rather to convey something of the essence of heavenly existence. By reference to architecture, John is making a much broader point: the creativity, vibrancy and lavish abundance of life in heaven is beyond compare with our earthly existence. Far from leaving behind our capacity for artistic creativity, our appreciation of beauty, and above all our delight in loving relationships, in the celestial city we will enter into the super-abundance of eternal life. Life beyond the grave is not a pale shadow of life on earth. Here is the pale shadow, there we will enter the fullness.

Jesus' resurrection and Paul's reflections upon its implications for all believers reinforce this positive understanding of heaven. In the resurrection appearances, Jesus is entirely capable of normal human activities: he meets his friends, he speaks and eats. And yet he is no longer confined within the space-time continuum of earthly existence. He can walk through walls and seems to appear and disappear at will. While such events are deeply inexplicable and mysterious, they clearly suggest a mode of existence that is richer, not poorer, than life on earth: a way of living that encompasses all that we can know at present, and yet with additional and remarkable new potentialities. Paul provides a series of striking and extreme contrasts to express the transcendent nature of resurrection life, like a seed which must be buried in the ground and die before it can be transformed into a full-grown plant (1 Cor. 15). We will be transposed, Paul argues, from perishable to imperishable, from dishonour to glory, from weakness to power. We will not leave behind bodily existence in order to become some kind of disembodied spirits, but rather we will enjoy a decisive and permanent exchange, from mortal existence with an earthly body to the extravagant abundance of eternal life with a spiritual body.

When we pray to our heavenly Father, the phrase is designed to quicken a longing for immortality, a hunger for heaven. Where God is, there we hope to be. This life, in all its capacity for wonder and pleasure, is but a foreshadowing, a season of preparation. This phrase is therefore brimful with future hope. To pray to our Father in heaven speaks not only of God's location, but of our ultimate destination.

Above all, in heaven our encounter with God will be direct,

unambiguous and uninterrupted. Then we will know as we are known, and grasp the fullness of God's merciful, eternal and triune love. Just as the phrase 'our Father in heaven' tells us something about God's eternal dwelling place, that higher dimension of spiritual existence to which we aspire, it also reveals a glorious consequence of the divine presence. Heaven is indeed where God is, and where we will enter into unrestricted encounter with the constantly available divine presence. But also, wherever we meet with God, there heaven is found. It was the presence of God in the burning bush that made an ordinary hillside become holy ground during Moses' historic encounter. It was the presence of the risen Christ that made the Damascus Road holy ground at the time of Saul's conversion. When we pray to our Father in heaven, we have the opportunity for a fresh encounter. As we meet with the Father, in that moment we enter the courts of heaven. As we look forward to the 'not yet' of heaven in all its fullness, we can enjoy a foretaste, a little of heaven come down to earth, even as we pray.

Personal reflection

How could you cultivate an increasing appetite for heaven?

5

Holy is your name

Holiness has been hijacked by negativity. In Jesus' day, the Pharisees thought they knew all about holiness. They not only sought to keep the law, they created countless extra rules and regulations. The theory was that if they fenced the law, and then stayed beyond the boundaries of their own additional legislation, they were sure to avoid offending God. Such was their obsession with legalistic details that they were scrupulous to tithe even the herbs from their gardens. And yet, faced with Jesus, they were entirely unable to recognise genuine goodness. All they could see was a danger to their religious authority, who needed to be opposed. Their lives were riddled with religious rules, their hearts plagued with coldness, envy and bitterness.

In Jesus we see a quite different conception of the heart of holiness. To be sure, when he challenged his opponents to identify a single breach of God's law, they were reduced to silence. Without bothering with the vast panoply of the Pharisees' additional regulations, he remained pure and true in all his ways. But genuine holiness is far more than avoiding forbidden actions. In the great ethical teaching of the Sermon on the Mount, so remarkably and comprehensively fulfilled in Jesus' own life, he called his followers to a positive holiness, to purity of heart and self-giving love.

The Old Testament call to holiness begins with the character of God: 'Be holy, even as I am holy.' Merely to say that God commits no sin is an impoverished definition of divine holiness. By definition God is free from all sin. Far more than that, God reveals himself in the pages of the Bible as one who is super-abundant in mercy and compassion, long in patience and slow to anger. Above all, during his crucifixion we see Jesus demonstrating the extravagant excesses of divine love; a love not restricted to his faithful followers, but reaching out to offer forgiveness even to his enemies. Perfect holiness certainly sets God apart from humanity, but not in a dour, cramped and legalistic negativity. We see in Jesus and in the Father that he reveals nothing of the so-called holiness of Pharisaism, with its instinctive disapproval of anything that gives men and women pleasure. Our God has none of the drab, grey, lacklustre, mean-minded attitudes of a supernatural kill-joy.

There is a wonderful *joie de vivre* in Jesus: he positively radiates abundance of life and revels in the pleasures of existence. His appreciation of the beauty of the natural world is unmistakable, just as much as his evident delight in any opportunity to enjoy a relaxing meal with friends. Perfect holiness does nothing to cramp Jesus' style. Far from reducing him to the half-life of the Pharisees, shrouded in legalistic nit-picking, Jesus' kind of holy living is a life worth living, bursting with vibrant vitality.

When we declare that God is holy, we are making several statements at once. It is a declaration of faith, that we believe in the unsullied purity and love of our Creator. It is an acceptance of biblical revelation, for through the Old Testament Law, Prophets and Wisdom, God is continually revealed in his holiness. At the same time, when we make Jesus' prayer our own, we are making an offering of praise. In describing his character, we ascribe to him the honour that is his due. We offer the worship of our heart and mind to the one who is all-worthy.

The Old Testament speaks of the song of creation. Like a transcendent orchestra, the entire universe joins, in its order and beauty, in a cosmic symphony of praise. The human contribution stands apart. Because we are fallen, with a built-in bias to selfishness and sin, our lives bring discord to the song of the universe. Still worse, in the way that we treat one another and despoil the planet, the human race is continually disfiguring the symphony of praise.

There is an immensely positive potential to the human contribution to the cosmic symphony. Most of the song of creation has no choice in its contribution, it just is: in its soaring grandeur, a snow-capped mountain cannot help but declare the praise of God, even so the delicate tracery of a butterfly's wings, the exquisite melodies of a nightingale's song, or the molten, burning beauty of a volcanic lava flow. Men and women have the freedom to take a leading part in the song or ignore it altogether. Here is a higher form of worship, considered and chosen rather than instinctive and automatic. When we declare God's holiness, the song of creation is immeasurably enriched with the voices of the self-aware and free.

A declaration of God's holiness means nothing if it is no more than fine words. If we genuinely enter into the worship of a holy God, our attitudes, words and behaviour will begin to express our genuine devotion to the God of purity and love. As we offer mercy and kindness to others, provide care for creation and seek to live in the way of the Sermon on the Mount, with purity of heart and self-giving love, we embrace the holiness of God. That is not to say that we can or will always get it right. But there must a willingness for our lifestyle to be brought into conformity with the God we say we serve. When our lips declare God's praise, but our lives show no expression of his holy love, the currency of worship has been debased. Our words become worthless.

Worship is a lifestyle, not mere verbal conformity. Worship is seven days a week, not merely on Sunday mornings. The more our lives are brought into harmony with the positive holiness of Jesus, the more we can experience the 'life in all its fullness' that our Master confidently promised his followers. In short, the more we worship, the more we gain fulfilment. Worship brings us into right relationship with our Creator. Part of our design and purpose is to give due praise to God. When this built-in purpose finds expression, in words and lifestyle, we are fulfilling our potential, expressing the creaturely appreciation that is a hallmark of our existence. The very act of expressing our worship is designed to do us good.

The instinct to express praise runs deep. Anyone with a passion for a pastime, from football to photography, fell-walking to knitting, will talk about it with enthusiasm. They don't need much prompting, and once they have started, there's often no holding them back! Even though we often cannot find the words to express our pleasure, we still want to talk. It seems that expressing our wonder, admiration or enjoyment somehow reinforces and deepens the experience. Sometimes when I am travelling alone I visit some glorious art gallery and my first thought is, 'I wish Claire were here to share this with me.' When I get home, I want to tell her about it, searching for the words to express my delight.

It is the same with something as simple and delicious as a bowl of strawberries. The natural human instinct is to declare our pleasure: 'I just love strawberries!' This represents something more than thanking the person who has prepared a meal. Our pleasures find fuller expression when we communicate appreciation or enthusiasm in words. At the root of this familiar experience is something at the heart of what it means to be human: we are created as worshipping beings. If we choose not to worship God, our natural instinct to worship will find other outlets. When we enter freely into heartfelt worship, we experience fulfilment. The expression of worship reinforces and completes our delight in life. That is not to say that we offer worship for what we can get out of it. Certainly not, for true worship is necessarily God-centred, doing no more than giving the Lord of Creation his just deserts. But there is an unmistakable spin-off. The more we enter into worship, the more we will appreciate life.

Prayer response

Pause to appreciate the goodness of God. How can you ensure thankfulness is an integral part of your daily lifestyle?

6

The name of God

It is a strange feeling to be eating in a restaurant far from home and hear someone call your name. Almost certainly they are calling out to someone else with the same name, but we are conditioned to react to being named. Almost involuntarily we look up, enquiringly and expectantly. Our name matters to us, and being called by name gives us a sense of identity and relationship.

Names meant much more in the ancient world than in the West at the end of the twentieth century. The meaning of names was well understood and taken seriously. A person's destiny was often thought to be determined by the choice of a name. To know someone's name was to know something very important about him or her. For example, Abram, which means 'exalted father', was renamed by God as Abraham, which means 'father of many'. His promised and long-awaited son was called Isaac, which means 'he laughs'.

It was not just the Israelites who took seriously the meaning of names and the personal identity they express and reinforce. Just as Elijah means 'Yahweh is God', the father of Jezebel, who actively sought to impose the worship of Baal among the Jews, was King Ethbaal of the Phoenicians, and his name meant 'Baal lives'. Although Jezebel's name has gone down in history to signify a woman of the worst repute, among the Phoenicians her name meant 'where is the prince?' That is, her name declared her to be a beauty fit for a king.

Among the Jews, the name had a quite different connotation, for it sounded like a Hebrew phrase that meant 'no dung'. The Jewish perspective on Jezebel was immediately quite different from the Phoenician!

God has many titles bestowed in the Old Testament. He is, for example, the Lord of hosts, the Provider, the Rock, the Sovereign Lord, and the God of Abraham, Isaac and Jacob. Each title describes some aspect of Israel's experience of their God. When Moses was trying to wriggle out of his call to lead Israel out of Egypt, he asked for something more – not merely a descriptive title derived from human experience but a direct revelation of the name of God. In response, God speaks his name, a word so sacred that the Jews traditionally use a substitute in the public reading of their Scriptures. Jahweh, traditionally translated as Jehovah, means 'I am who I am'. It also has a future resonance, 'I will be what I will be'. The mysterious and sacred name of God has many implications.

- It speaks of God's *self-existence*: divine life has no source outside itself, no dependence upon others.
- It speaks of God's *eternality*: divine life exists in the timeless present, beyond the constraints of finite existence within the dimension of time.
- It speaks of God's *otherness*: even as God reveals the essence of divinity, the mystery of divine otherness is undiminished.
- It speaks of God's *self-disclosure*: the name of God could not be unmasked by theological deduction but must be revealed.
- It speaks of God's *willingness to communicate*: he accommodates himself within the constraints of human language, in order to reveal himself with maximum clarity and accessibility.

If Moses had only enjoyed an intuitive encounter with God, however remarkable, others would have received no more than a second-hand impression of the nature of God. But when God reveals his name, he opens up new understanding, new opportunities for worship and relationship, not exclusively for Moses, but for all who call upon his name.

God's concern for his name and its honour is a constant refrain of the Old Testament. In the Ten Commandments it is emphasised that his name must not be taken in vain. When Solomon's Temple is built, God graces the building with his presence, yet emphasises his transcendence. The Temple is not the dwelling place of God himself, as if he could be restricted in space and time like the gods and idols of other nations. Rather, it is the dwelling place of the divine name: that is, his self-revelation. In Ezekiel's prophecies, the reason why God will once again come to Israel's rescue, beyond the Babylonian exile, is not because they deserve it, nor as a result of the covenant, which they have continually breached, but rather 'for the honour of my name'.

To honour God's name is therefore a prayer rich with Jewish resonance. By his self-revelation, even of his name, God has made himself accessible to his worshippers. By his actions, both in the order and beauty of creation and in his interventions in the history of Israel, God has demonstrated himself to be worthy of his name and deserving of our worship. We are therefore invited to declare our creaturely dependence and put ourselves in right relationship with the one whose name is worthy of all praise.

The New Testament adds a new dimension to honouring the name of God which has incalculable importance. In ancient Greek, the word *kurios* – 'lord' – had many levels of meaning. It was a polite term of address in everyday conversation, the equivalent of 'sir'. It also acknowledged someone's status as a leader or teacher. When the Roman Empire sought to introduce emperor worship, the confession 'Caesar is Lord' was taken to express not merely the authority of the Emperor, but even his divinity. For the Jews the word had an additional significance, because in the Greek translation of the Hebrew Scriptures, the Septuagint, the word '*kurios*' was used to represent the name of God.

There are many names associated with Jesus in the New Testament. He is Jesus, which means 'the Lord saves'. Recalling Isaiah's prophecy of the virginal conception, he is identified as Immanuel, meaning 'God with us'. He is Christ in Greek, which is the equivalent of Messiah in Hebrew, meaning 'God's anointed one'. He is the Son of God and the Son of Man. But above all he is Lord. When Jesus is addressed in the Gospels as 'Lord', it may sometimes signify no more than customary respect for a rabbi. But the first Christians were well aware of the deeper layers of meaning when they confessed in one of the earliest creeds, 'Jesus is Lord'. Here is more than a statement about the authority of Jesus' teaching and the willing obedience of his followers. Nothing less than the name of God is conferred upon Jesus: the divinity of the Son is declared in the confession of his Lordship. For the Christian believer, to honour the name of God is inextricably tied up with honouring Jesus, whose right to the name of God we gladly confess. The Lord's Prayer becomes not only the prayer given to his followers by Jesus, but also a prayer in which, alongside the Father, the name of the Son is honoured and glorified.

Prayer response

Take a moment of prayerful reflection upon one or more of the names of Jesus.

7

Bible Meditation

ISAIAH 42:1–4

Isaiah's servant songs have several layers of meaning: they speak of Isaiah's own ministry; they describe the calling of Israel; supremely they prophesy the suffering servanthood of Christ; and they describe the resultant priorities of the Church, called to follow in the ways of the Master. This particular song emphasises the faithfulness of God, shown first towards his servant and then expressed through his servant to the world.

Servants are often disregarded by those who have hired them, but God describes his servant in four positive ways:

- God upholds him – providing protection, strength and encouragement;
- God has chosen him – affirming his specialness;
- God delights in him – taking active pleasure in the servant;
- and God puts his Spirit upon him – lavishing his loving presence upon the servant.

We can read these words as a description of the unique standing of Jesus, but also as a remarkable invitation to parent–child intimacy with the God whom we serve.

The servant's task is described in three ways. For the Christian, these qualities express the character of Christ towards the world, and also beckon us towards a fuller imitation of Christ in our own daily living.

- He will not shout, cry out or raise his voice in the street. There is nothing strident, aggressive, hostile or bullying about Jesus. Our tone of voice often reveals our attitude of heart towards those with whom we are speaking.
- He will not break a bruised reed or snuff out a smouldering wick. Where others may see only weakness and failure, readily rejecting someone as 'not up to the mark', Jesus sees potential, and patiently works to bring out the best in us. We also need to learn to become those who are known for our willingness to believe in others rather than impatiently dismissing them out of hand.
- He will bring forth justice with faithfulness, without faltering or falling into discouragement. Impulsive enthusiasts adopt a five-minute campaign for justice but drift into indifference when the going gets tough. Jesus is iron-willed in his determination, implacable in his resolve to pursue the full implementation of divine justice upon the face of the earth. Our confidence in this divine resolve can then inspire us to continue to work for high moral standards and social justice, not easily losing heart when faced with indifference, misrepresentation or even hostility to our championing of biblical values.

Pause to reflect on the threefold implication of this passage:

- the character of God expressed and revealed in Christ;
- the disposition of God towards his world and Church, and also towards us personally;
- the example of Christ, which inspires us to pursue a lifestyle that gives expression to the divine character and priorities.

DEVOTIONAL POEMS

Now we must praise the Ruler of Heaven,
The might of the Lord and his purpose of mind,
The work of the Glorious Father; for he
God Eternal, established each wonder,
He, Holy Creator, first fashioned the heavens
As a roof for the children of earth.
And then our Guardian, the Everlasting Lord,
Adorned this middle earth for men.
Praise the Almighty King of Heaven.

Caedmon, 7th century

Though young, yet wise, though small, yet strong;
though man, yet God he is;
As wise he knows, as strong he can,
as God he loves to bless.
His knowledge rules, his strength defends,
his love doth cherish all;
His birth our joy, his life our light,
his death our end of thrall.

Robert Southwell, 1561–95

Glorious the sun in mid career;
Glorious the assembled fires appear;
Glorious the comet's train:
Glorious the trumpet and alarm;
Glorious the almighty stretched out arm;
Glorious the enraptured main:

Glorious the northern lights astream;
Glorious the song, when God's the theme;
Glorious the thunder's roar:
Glorious hosanna from the den;
Glorious the catholic amen;
Glorious the martyr's gore:

Glorious – more glorious is the crown
Of him that brought salvation down
By meekness called thy Son;
Thou that stupendous truth believed,
And now the matchless deed's achieved,
DETERMINED, DARED, AND DONE.

Christopher Smart, 1722–71

As due by many titles I resign
My self to thee, O God, first I was made
By thee, and for thee, and when I was decay'd
Thy blood bought that, the which before was thine,
I am thy son, made with thy self to shine,
Thy servant, whose pains thou hast still repaid,
Thy sheep, thine Image, and till I betray'd
My self, a temple of thy Spirit divine;
Why doth the devil then usurp on me?
Why doth he steal nay ravish that's thy right?
Except thou rise and for thine own work fight,
Oh I shall soon despair, when I do see
That thou lov'st mankind well, yet wilt not choose me,
And Satan hates me, yet is loth to lose me.

John Donne, 1572–1631

CHAPTER II

YOUR KINGDOM COME, YOUR WILL BE DONE, ON EARTH AS IT IS IN HEAVEN

Thy kingdom come;
thy will be done;
on earth as it is in heaven

GRACE

My stock lies dead, and no increase
Doth my dull husbandry improve:
O let thy graces without cease
Drop from above!

If still the sun should hide his face,
Thy house would but a dungeon prove,
Thy works night's captives: O let grace
Drop from above!

The dew doth ev'ry morning fall;
And shall the dew outstrip thy Dove?
The dew, for which grass cannot call,
Drop from above.

Death is still working like a mole,
And digs my grave at each remove:
Let grace work too, and on my soul
Drop from above.

Sin is still hammering my heart
Unto a hardness void of love:
Let suppling grace, to cross his art,
Drop from above.

O come! For thou dost know the way:
Or if to me thou wilt not move,
Remove me, where I need not say,
Drop from above.

George Herbert

1

Rule, righteousness and right relations

There are few kingdoms left in the modern Western world. Even those countries that have retained a monarchy of sorts emphasise their democratic credentials. In the UK the majority of the population continue to express an instinctive sense of respect, loyalty and admiration for the royal family that sets them apart from any politicians. But the national aspiration is to be a modern and effective democracy, reflected in the move finally to abolish seats in the Lords for hereditary peers. Few, if any, could seriously wish to revert to the non-democratic kingdom of the medieval and Tudor eras.

At the dawn of the twenty-first century, has talk of God's kingdom had its day? Is it a way of speaking that is too alien, too anachronistic to have meaning in the modern Church? And does talk of Christ as King inevitably lead to authoritarian leaders, emphasising their own right to 'rule' over the Church?

The language of the kingdom was forever on Jesus' lips. It was his preferred way of speaking about the new way of living that he offered. For the Jews under Roman rule, the appeal must have been immediate. Their nation had been established by divine initiative, securing their liberation from slavery in Egypt by a series of miraculous interventions. They had laid claim to the Promised Land during the period of conquest with a series of battles often marked by prayer and extraordinarily dramatic success: minuscule armies had defeated huge numbers; city walls had fallen at a trumpet blast; the Jews had developed an air of invincibility. At first the tribes had been led by men and women known as judges, but in due course, Samuel the prophet, who seems also to have functioned as the last of the judges, accepted with some reluctance on behalf of God the demand of the people for a king. Prompted by God, Samuel selected Saul as the first king, a man with the stature and presence of a Hollywood super-hero. When Saul's life began to fall apart, David was anointed as his successor, and the Davidic kingdom pushed the borders of the Jewish land to their greatest extent. David's son and successor, Solomon, continued the success story, building a magnificent temple and palace that consolidated the status of Jerusalem as the centre of political and religious life. Solomon's wealth and wisdom won for him and his nation an unprecedented renown throughout the Middle East. No longer newcomers at the international table, the former nomads and slaves now enjoyed a new-found identity as a kingdom that was established and respected, stable and secure.

Some sporting stars' early triumphs are emblazoned across the newspaper headlines, but their later careers fail to live up to expectations. In a similar way, the Jewish kingdom peaked early. First there was civil war after Solomon's death, resulting in a division into two kingdoms that was never healed. Then there was a wretched inclination to idolatry, with many kings in both kingdoms leading their people in pursuit of the common gods of the Middle East: Baal the macho god of fertility, Asherah who was a Mother Earth goddess, and Moloch, whose perverse and voracious appetite was for the fiery sacrifice of children.

After the time of Solomon, the Jews were always at risk from the latest empire of the Middle East. Like a tortoise withdrawing into its shell, their borders shrank back from the greater extent of the Davidic kingdom. With each wave of imperial conquest, the Jews looked more vulnerable. The Assyrians eventually destroyed the northern kingdom in 722 BC, then marched up to the very gates of Jerusalem to lay siege to the capital, before eventually being overcome by a sudden plague. The northern kingdom then disappeared from the face of the earth, and the southern kingdom struggled on until the Babylonians eventually overcame the Assyrians and then seized the only remaining kingdom of the Jews, with Jerusalem falling in 586 BC. The Persians succeeded the Babylonians, and the Jews were finally permitted to return home under Ezra and Nehemiah. Alexander the Great was the next major imperialist to march through the Middle East, and his successors divided his single-generation empire into three, which in turn were overtaken by the Roman Empire. For the Jews, this represented several hundred years of political bagatelle, during which they were almost inevitably subject to the next imperial power. Their experience of independence, international glory, and the line of Davidic kings, receded ever further into the remote and seemingly irretrievable past.

After so many generations of subservience to successive empires, by the time of Jesus the longing for an independent Jewish kingdom was moving, perhaps inevitably, in two contrary directions. Some had more or less given up hope that the Davidic glory days could ever return. Others burned with a fierce longing for the all-conquering Son of David, the Messiah promised by the prophets, who would surely overthrow the Romans and Herod, their puppet king, and establish the kingdom of God on earth that would know no end.

We can identify four distinct strands of Jewish thinking about the kingdom of God.

- The first celebrated the *intervention of God in Jewish history*: at every stage he had worked mightily to advance the cause of his covenant people.
- The second strand was *political*, emphasising Israel as an independent nation established in its rightful lands.
- Both the law and the prophets emphasised that the third essential strand was *ethical*: the God of the covenant demanded a nation

that expressed the divine priorities of love, purity and justice. Because the kingdom of Israel was understood to be God's own kingdom, the people were called to express the righteousness of God, both as individuals and in national, public life. The prophets railed not only against idolatry, which they considered a betrayal of the covenant and the religious equivalent of adultery, but also against the exploitation of the poor. In particular, the privileges of living in the kingdom of the covenant brought responsibilities to care for widows, orphans and foreign refugees, and no excuse was acceptable for exploitation, whether by traders, employers or those who enjoyed the power and trappings of amassed wealth.

- The fourth strand was *futuristic*, holding onto the promise of the prophets that God's purposes for the human race had not been swept aside by the apparently irresistible might of these succeeding world powers. Emperors and their armies of conquest and occupation would not have the last word in human history.

When Jesus took up the theme of the kingdom of God, he deftly repositioned the four established strands of its significance. For Jesus, the emphasis upon the intervention of God now had both a present and a future dimension. In the present, the kingdom is breaking in upon everyday living, as the sick are healed and good news is preached to the poor. Jesus therefore invited the crowds to make a response of repentance and faith and so enter fully into the present dimension of the kingdom. At the same time, he spoke of the future consummation of the kingdom, the decisive coming of God to usher in both final judgment and the unassailable fullness of the eternal kingdom. The ethical strand is intensified, supremely in the Sermon on the Mount. For Jesus, the life of the kingdom requires a radical intensity of self-giving love towards God and one another, a positive holiness expressed in purity of heart, and a willingness to be the servant of all. As to the future strand, we have already seen that Jesus emphasises the future consummation but also the present coming of the kingdom. The present availability of the kingdom becomes a foretaste of all that is promised. The future breaks into the present. The now dimension of living in the kingdom becomes a foretaste of all that is yet to come.

Jesus' emphasis shifts the ground fundamentally, rather than intensifying the existing Jewish understanding, when he defines the location of the kingdom. Wherever there is a response of living faith, there the kingdom of God is found. This kingdom is 'among you', visible in a community of faith, but also 'within you', an inward responsiveness to God. Jesus strips away the political dimension of the kingdom. Entry is now by personal faith, not by the birthright of nationality. Its borders are denoted by the obedience of discipleship, not by the territory under the control of a human king. The rule of God is direct, not through a human king. The geography of the kingdom is the terrain of the human heart, not the villages of Galilee or the Jordan Valley. Unconstrained by location, nationality, or generation, the rule of God finds expression wherever there is a response of faith.

Jesus takes familiar expectations and super-charges them with the prospect of God's immediate and available presence. His way of life is not merely a code of high conduct: he calls us to faithful surrender to the present rule of God. The kingdom is both an ideal and an experience, a future hope that can also be experienced as a present reality. As a deep-sea diver depends on the micro-environment of his oxygen supply, the disciple of Jesus can live in the environment of the kingdom, not merely serving God at a distance but immersed in the ruling presence of the Lord of the cosmos.

In a secularised society, we are conditioned to live much of the time without any reference to God. But the promise of Jesus is timeless: the kingdom of God has broken out upon the face of the earth and can now be entered and experienced. God's ruling presence is among us and also within us, as we tune in, by faith, to this hidden and higher dimension of human existence. Beyond the material is found the spiritual: and there we can discover and explore the infinitely rewarding kingdom without borders, the spiritual environment which is accessible from every possible location on planet earth.

Prayer response

Pause for a moment to recognise that you are living in the presence of the kingdom of God.

2

Jesus, the kingdom bringer

Jesus does far more than proclaim the kingdom of God. He brings it. After John the Baptist had been imprisoned, he experienced a crisis of faith, wondering whether Jesus really was the one for whom he had been preparing the way, or whether the people still needed to wait for God's Promised One. He sent word to Jesus, asking for reassurance. In reply, Jesus confidently cited an Old Testament prophecy that had found fulfilment in his ministry:

> *The blind receive sight, the lame walk, those who have leprosy are cured, the deaf hear, the dead are raised, and the good news is preached to the poor.*
>
> Matthew 11:5

Jesus plainly considered the evidence to be conclusive: he was indeed God's uniquely anointed servant.

The early chapters of Mark's Gospel are punctuated by a refrain of amazement at the authority of Jesus. The people were astounded at his authority as a teacher, for he was unlike any teacher they had ever heard before (Mark 1:22). They were astounded at his authority over evil spirits who obeyed without delay his command to depart their human habitation (Mark 1:27). They were astounded at his healing ministry and his boldness in declaring sins forgiven (Mark 2:7, 12).

They were astounded at his readiness to eat with the non-religious poor, who were known disparagingly as 'sinners', and also with tax collectors who were making money out of collaboration with the Roman occupying force (Mark 2:16). When a storm blew up suddenly, as they always have on Lake Galilee, they were astonished that he even had authority over the wind and waves (Mark 4:41).

Time and again Jesus exercised the authority of the kingdom of God, which claims rightful dominion over every aspect of human existence. Here is no cool and detached teacher of theoretical ethics, offering a mere theory of right living. Jesus was directly involved with his followers, so that they knew with certainty that they were befriended and loved. More than that, the lifestyle he commended and lived grew directly out of an awareness of the equipping presence of the rule of God. The immensity, intensity and constancy of the Father's love empowers the citizens of his kingdom to keep on living in the way of love.

When some dared to suggest that Jesus' power to cast out demons could be attributed to Satan, his response was robust. His opposition to Satan demonstrated the power of the kingdom of God, evicting the denizens of darkness. He claimed to drive out demons 'by the finger of God', and declared that this direct demonstration of divine authority was conclusive evidence that 'the kingdom of God has come to you' (Luke 11:20). Jesus' claim is double: in his actions, God himself is directly at work; and the coming of the kingdom is demonstrated conclusively in his saving authority for those damaged and ensnared by the power of evil. Quite simply, in Jesus' ministry, the kingdom of God is manifest.

What is true of Jesus' ministry is true of his teaching. Other rabbis would quote Moses and the rabbinical tradition with due deference. Jesus repeatedly asserted the supreme authority of his own teaching, in such phrases as 'Truly, truly I say to you' and 'You have heard it said . . . but I say'. When calling his disciples, rather than making an invitation to follow God, he once again presumes to speak in the first person of God's own authority: 'Follow me.'

Jesus' remarkable claims for himself are unambiguous. He not only teaches about the kingdom of God, he embodies it. If we want to see what the kingdom looks like in action, there is no better place to turn than the life and ministry of Jesus. Similarly, if we want to know more about the character of God, according to Jesus there is no better place to look than the life of the Son. Jesus is God made touchable: the invisible is seen, the mystery unveiled, and the eternal kingdom takes human form.

In Jesus' parables he does more than teach about the kingdom and invite a response of repentance, faith and obedience. The parables provoke questions not simply about God's kingdom, but about Jesus himself. The response of faith is a response not just to the Father, but also to Jesus. More than the herald, he is the bringer of the kingdom, the one who makes possible its new in-breaking into space and time. To reject Jesus is to be excluded from the kingdom, to accept him is to accept the warm embrace of the Father's realm.

To pray about 'your kingdom' is therefore to use a phrase that points in two directions. It speaks of the Father's kingdom, the rule of God on the face of the earth. But it also speaks of the Son, the bringer of the kingdom, who shows us what the kingdom is like and brings the beginning of the end of time, the foretaste of eternity, as he announces the dawn of the fulfilment of God's promises.

The apostolic generation had a sensitive manoeuvre to make for the sake of effective Gentile mission. Without Jewish background knowledge of the Old Testament, a phrase that was rich in meaning risked becoming incomprehensible. And the Roman authorities might easily misinterpret kingdom talk to signify a rebellion being hatched against imperial domination. These factors at least partly explain why the apostolic writings outside the Gospels make much less use of the phrase 'kingdom of God'. Instead, Jesus himself is centre stage, the risen Lord who has come in human flesh. In short, while Jesus proclaims that the kingdom has come and is yet to come, after his resurrection and ascension, his followers proclaim the risen and coming King. To understand the character of the King is to grasp the priorities of the kingdom. To yield to the King is to enter his kingdom. Like love and marriage and a horse and carriage in the old song, Jesus and the kingdom of God are an indivisible pair – you can't have one without the other.

Personal reflection

In what part of your life do you most readily drift away from submission to the kingship of Jesus?

3

Your will be done

Hebrew poetry loves repetition. Where traditional poetry in many European languages rhymes words, ancient Hebrew poetry rhymes meaning. Poetry has been defined as what is lost in translation. But Hebrew poetry is remarkably translatable: the rhyming of meaning crosses the language barrier far more effectively than the rhythms and rhymes of individual words. The Psalms show us the standard Hebraic patterns of meaning rhymes. There is the simple parallel, in which the same statement is made in different words. There is the intensifying parallel, in which the second statement is stronger than the first. There is the negative parallel, in which the second statement confirms the first by contradicting its opposite. There is the negative intensifier, in which the second statement contradicts a statement more strongly stated than the first. And so the more elaborate parallelisms proliferate.

At this point in the Lord's Prayer, Jesus' phrasing is characteristically Jewish. There is a close parallel between God's kingdom coming and his will being done. The full expression of God's will is, after all, nothing less than the coming of his kingdom, expressed in loving, right relationships, righteous living before God, and just and fair treatment for all.

This parallel phrase does, however, raise a problem and emphasise personal application. The problem concerns the will of God, or, more precisely, how to reconcile God's sovereign will and human freedom. Those who give exclusive emphasis to divine sovereignty can cite scriptures in defence of their position: Ezekiel continually emphasised God's sovereign will, shaping the destiny of the human race; Paul speaks of a God who has predestined those he saves; and Jesus speaks of us not choosing him, but him choosing us, and of the Father drawing us to himself. Pushed to an extreme position, such statements can strip human beings of all dignity and freedom, reducing us to a robotic helplessness, continuing in sin on automatic pilot unless God reprograms us, in which case we automatically become his devoted servants.

Those who give exclusive emphasis to human free will can equally cite scriptures in defence of their position: Genesis emphasises human freedom to choose obedience or disobedience before the fall; Paul urges believers to choose the ways of God, actively removing their old lifestyle and clothing themselves with newness of life in Christ; and, of course, Jesus invites people to make an active choice to repent, believe and follow him.

So how do we reconcile these two strands of biblical emphasis? It is always tempting to be selective with the evidence, explaining away those emphases that do not conform to our preferred approach. For example, some redefine 'predestination' as a passive foreknowledge. God stands outside the stream of time, and from the vantage point of eternity he can see all of time at once. He therefore knows the beginning from the end simply by means of keen observation. The equal and opposite error is to attempt to explain away all emphasis upon human choice and freedom. The logic of predestination is pursued beyond the limits of the Bible, notably with two proposals. First, it is suggested that God must predestine some to eternal damnation – a cruel and cold rationalistic deduction that provoked prolonged agonies of heart in William Cowper, the great hymn writer, for fear that he was one destined to be damned. Second, it is suggested that, since God had already predestined the saved and the damned, the death of Christ was a limited atonement, restricting its power to save to the closed circle of the positively predestined. Just as one extreme grouping must water down 'predestination', the other must water down the New Testament emphasis upon God so loving the 'world' that he gave his only Son. 'World', they explain, really means the company of those who will be saved. Such creative reinterpretation results in a theological system that is certainly self-consistent, but much more neat and simplistic than biblical revelation.

Western patterns of thinking have been profoundly shaped by classical Greek philosophy and Enlightenment rationalism. Faced with an apparent contradiction, we instinctively attempt to explain away one of the dissonant factors, in this case human freedom or divine sovereignty. Alternatively we attempt to create some kind of synthesis, accepting a limited percentage of each element, so that in this case we may attempt to suggest a 'balanced position', in which people are partly free and God is partly sovereign. The result of such approaches is that we tend to castrate either freedom or sovereignty, or even emasculate both at once.

Hebraic thought is remarkably untroubled by such tensions. Rather than looking for a synthesis that oversimplifies reality, Jesus and his first followers embraced dialectical thinking: they affirmed simultaneously the sovereignty of God and the freedom, responsibility and dignity of human beings. Rather than embracing one truth at the expense of the other, or looking for some mid-point of compromise, they simultaneously affirmed both extremes. In some mysterious way, the full truth of these two perspectives is retained, so that divine sovereignty and human freedom do not clash, but rather reinforce one another. Thus, in a single saying, Jesus can affirm both truths unreservedly, emphasising both the prerogative of divine selectivity and yet an invitation to all to come to Christ:

All things have been committed to me by my Father. No one knows the Son except the Father, and no one knows the Father except the

> *Son and those to whom the Son chooses to reveal him. Come to me, all you who are weary and burdened, and I will give you rest.*
>
> Matthew 11:27–8

Once we get beyond the anxieties that can sometimes be provoked by the paradoxical interlocking of sovereignty and freedom, we enter into the safe place of praying for God's will to be fulfilled in our lives. Jesus' phrase encourages a willing, personal surrender to the good purposes of our Father in heaven, not a robotic muttering that verbalises an inescapable reality, in which every last detail of life is predetermined, including our use of this prayer. To pray for God's will to be done is meant to be a prayer that provides peace not consternation, willing obedience not an abandonment of freedom and responsibility.

A baby instinctively closes his hand upon the finger of an adult. The entire grasp clasps a single adult finger. When the adult responds and closes a hand in return, the baby's fingers, hand and even the arm are entirely enclosed. Even so, my hold on God will sometimes seem very weak, and yet the Father's hold on me is strong, secure and safe. We are safe in the grip of grace. To surrender to God is not to yield with a sense of resignation to the unavoidable and implacable iron will of determinism. It is to embrace the obedience that leads to perfect peace.

We never outgrow this yielding to Jesus, but we easily drift from our moorings. The demands of daily life naturally absorb our energy, and our priorities can shift imperceptibly. Our favourite TV programmes present a perspective on life that may be insightful or enjoyable, but is almost inevitably less than fully Christian. Just as an orchestra must retune their instruments before they are ready for a concert performance, every time we pray 'Your will be done', we surrender ourselves anew to the Lordship of Christ and invite him to retune our lives, conforming us once again to his priorities and to the imitation of his character. We declare our allegiance, our willingness to serve and follow, and our preparedness to accept change in our lives, both inwardly and outwardly, for the sake of the Master.

Prayer response

Express afresh your unconditional surrender to God's good purposes, that your life may be a daily instrument of divine love.

4

The present coming of the kingdom

After days of teaching and healing down by the lakeside, Jesus made a habit of withdrawing to secluded places. He recharged his spiritual batteries by spending time alone with God. This was not selfishness or self-indulgence, nor a distraction from the practical ministry among the crowds. He needed time alone with God in order to be equipped to keep on serving others to the full. We need to learn to be still before God in prayer, rather than giving over all our praying to an endless and exhausting list of requests. (The practice of God's presence and the discipline of stillness are among the dimensions of prayer explored in the companion volume to this book, *Walking with God*.)

Just as there are times when the best way to pray is in seclusion, there are also times when we need to pray with a newspaper in our hands. To pray for the present coming of God's kingdom is a life-embracing prayer. In recent years, many churches have overthrown a rigid and formulaic approach to prayer that had become too formal and predictable. But in the rush to informality and spontaneity we can run the risk of a severely malnourished prayer life. Just as modern life is consumerist – what's in it for me? – the contemporary Western Church can become self-centred, indifferent to the needs of society and the world beyond the immediate sphere of our family and the local church. I am amazed and saddened by the number of churches that fail on a regular basis to pick up in public prayer on the great issues, opportunities and crises that dominate the headlines. Most Christians undoubtedly watch the news on TV or buy a daily newspaper, so the congregation is not entirely indifferent and uninformed. But life has been compartmentalised, so that those who watch the news have been losing the habit to pray about the news.

For some right-wing evangelicals, there is still a suspicion of the 'social gospel', fearing that any emphasis upon righteousness and justice in society might water down the 'real' gospel. Such people would never have invited many of the Old Testament prophets as visiting preachers! For some charismatics, the gospel is narrowed by pietistic prejudices. Prayer is about me and God, and perhaps the Church, but is rarely allowed to extend to society and the world. This narrowness is not the logical consequence of either evangelical or charismatic convictions. The evangelical who takes the Bible seriously will recognise the all-embracing righteous demands of the kingdom of God. The charismatic who takes the Holy Spirit seriously will recognise that the Old Testament prophets often have more to say about society than about Temple worship. I remember talking with David Sheppard about this during his time as Bishop of Liverpool, when I was editing his great book *Bias to the Poor*. He observed that if we curtail our concept of authentic prophecy to words for the Church and words of personal blessing, we have effectively hacked out of our Bibles huge chunks of Old Testament prophecy.

To take seriously praying through the headlines brings its own risks. When Margaret Thatcher fell from power, I came across prayer meetings in two Baptist churches, one in a Tory stronghold in Berkshire, one in a solidly Labour former mining area in South Yorkshire. The southern church held a special prayer meeting to give thanks for the Iron Lady's time in office, and to pray for mercy on the country when she had been dumped so suddenly by her own party. The northern church also gave thanks – that their prayers of many years had finally been answered and that the years of right-wing extremism and indifference to the working classes had at last been brought to an end. One prayed that God would spare his judgment from a parliament that had removed such a wondrous woman from office; the other thanked God that his judgment had finally been executed in her removal. No doubt the living God can cope more easily than a politically divided congregation, when we blur the line between biblical conviction and personal political prejudice!

The most awkward instance that I have encountered was when an African country was on the brink of civil war. A woman in the congregation was from the majority tribal grouping who had been suppressed by a tyrannical military regime: she prayed for justice, liberation and a return to democracy. A man from the minority tribal grouping of the government was also present, and so he promptly prayed for God to stay the hand of those who sought violence and revolution. It was like two party political broadcasts: civil war by prayer proxy! Such moments inevitably require some deft diplomatic footwork by the person leading the service. But they should certainly not give us any excuse to avoid praying for issues where controversy rages and chasms of prejudice divide opposing perspectives.

One of the hardest themes for prayer is when we are faced with an intractable social crisis. Like a deep-rooted weed in the garden that refuses to die out, we pray for a situation knowing full well that many have been praying for years, often with little evidence of progress. In Britain, many have struggled to persist in prayer for peace in Northern Ireland. In the States, many have struggled to persist in prayer over the race divisions and the crisis of social exclusion in the ghettos. Around the world, many have agonised over the steadily increasing numbers of drug addicts, the massive escalation in the numbers of abortions, the need for lasting peace with justice in the Middle East, and the unwillingness of developed countries to take decisive and radical action to deal with the obscenity of third-world debt. How do we manage to carry on praying when there is little or no evidence of improvement?

Three motivations can keep us praying and keep at bay the enemies of hope, namely resignation or cynicism, despair or even disgust. First, we pray because we must. No matter how hopeless the situation, how seemingly ineradicable the problem, the compassion of Christ quickens us to persevere in prayer. Second, we pray because of answered prayer. Many prayed for South Africa for years, hoping against hope that the apartheid regime would come to an end and that power would be transferred to the majority population without massive loss of life in a civil war. Of course there are continuing and deep-rooted problems in that country, but for many Christians, the hand-over to Nelson Mandela's presidency was nothing less than a miraculous answer to prayer. Third, we pray because Christian hope is resolute. As George Carey once observed, Christians have reason to be the most optimistic of all people. We face squarely the harsh realities and inevitable consequences of human sinfulness, but yet we live in confident hope. Jesus has initiated the age of God's kingdom, which has the capacity and authority to push back the boundaries of darkness and despair; Jesus' resurrection declares the triumph of goodness over suffering, sin and death; Jesus' promised return will see the complete eradication of evil and the full enactment of his kingdom of love. Whatever the apparent reasons to give up praying for the needs of this world, especially the hard situations of war and tyranny, famine and poverty, there are more than enough reasons in the Christian faith to motivate us to be steadfast in prayer.

The kingdom finds expression in a just society and a loving lifestyle, but at the heart of Jesus' proclamation is the need and opportunity for a response of personal faith to the one who makes the coming of the kingdom possible. Many Christians groan inwardly at the very mention of evangelism. Some wonder whether it is something too awful to do to a non-Christian friend. Others may not have any non-Christian friends anyway. We need to remind ourselves that Jesus did not stay locked away in a synagogue, preaching his heart out and waiting for people to attend a meeting. He took the gospel onto the home turf of outsiders, declaring the good news in imaginative ways that they could easily understand and giving them every opportunity to make a response of personal faith.

There was no hype, pressure, showmanship or manipulation about Jesus. He not only declared good news, but his character and methods of proclamation were also very good news indeed. Jesus' approach was fresh, creative and relevant, and we have no excuse for anything less in our evangelistic programmes. His preaching gives us a charter for experiment and exploration, using every available means of contemporary communication. His style was often open ended, leaving people with questions at the end of a wonderfully captivating story. Even so, we need to captivate hearts and minds, without feeling that no 'gospel presentation' is complete without a prolonged 'altar call'. Before we can persuade non-Christians to attend our evangelistic events, we have to persuade one another that we really can deliver programmes that are cringe-free and seeker sensitive.

The Alpha initiative provides many insights into what works well in contemporary evangelism.

- There is a meal, so the event does not feel overly religious and takes place in a social environment more familiar to many non-Christians than a worship service.
- There is an opportunity to build friendship, which meets the need to belong and also gives non-Christians an opportunity to decide whether Christians really do inhabit the same planet as the rest of the human race.
- There is a weekly talk within strict time constraints, designed to be accessible, practical, jargon-free and shot through with humour and illustrations.
- The individual sessions are complete without a weekly appeal, which makes sure people do not feel pressured into a premature response and gives them time to feel their way around the often unfamiliar terrain of the Christian faith.

- There is a steady exposure to different Bible passages, so that people are gradually moved beyond the biblical illiteracy that characterises this generation of Western Europeans.
- There are discussion groups, so that people can enjoy an interactive learning experience. This connects with modern styles of teaching at school and at college, and so is more familiar than the traditional Christian style of preaching without discussion.
- The groups also affirm people's autonomy: they are free to express their own opinions, ask any questions they like, and make a journey towards settled convictions and personal, living faith in their own time and way.
- There is a reasoned defence of the gospel, but also an opportunity to encounter God in personal experience, particularly during the Holy Spirit weekend. The course seeks to provide an opportunity for us to engage in a search for God with our whole being – neither switching off our minds nor engaging in an exclusively theoretical enquiry.

Inevitably Alpha is not for every church. Although huge numbers have found it the most successful evangelistic endeavour for many years, some are bound to feel that their particular emphasis requires a different approach. But these factors that give Alpha its remarkable cultural accessibility are entirely transferable, and could readily be adapted for other evangelistic enterprises, and even for our continuing discipleship programmes.

There are times when it is not enough to verbalise a prayer. When we ask God for the present coming of his kingdom, we implicate ourselves in the request. Those who pray for a better way of life in this generation must be willing to be part of God's solution. This simple phrase in Jesus' prayer is no less than life changing. It calls us to a radical reordering of our priorities, for its implications include financial generosity towards the poor, practical acts of compassion towards the needy, campaigning for justice, loving God and one another, and also the task of evangelism. If you are not willing to get your hands dirty in practical action, it is probably best not to pray for God's kingdom to advance in this generation.

Prayer response

Spend some moments praying through today's news headlines.

5

The future coming of the kingdom

The kingdom of God has several distinctive time zones. It has been inaugurated on earth in the coming of Christ. We pray for its present-day expression and advance. And we anticipate its future consummation in glory. The coming of the kingdom therefore operates in three tenses: it has come, it is coming and it will come.

Some Christians spill unnecessary ink and engage in fruitless controversy over the details of the end times. While some believers have altogether lost sight of the promised return of Christ, others seem to think of practically nothing else. History warns us that the period around the turn of the millennium will be ripe for a plague of end-times speculation. The kind of mindset that leads some people to devote many years to complex conspiracy theories about the death of Marilyn Monroe, John F. Kennedy or Princess Diana, and causes others to propose elaborate schemes by which governments are concealing the 'truth about UFOs', seems to motivate some Christians to develop blueprints and timetables that spell out a detailed schedule of the last days before Christ's return. Despite Jesus' own explicit disapproval of such schemes – he explained that the time could be known by the Father alone – some find the prospect of hidden knowledge, gleaned from 'cracking the code' of prophetic symbolism, to be an almost irresistible prospect. Judging from the book sales, for some speculators it becomes a crock of gold, won from the pockets of the gullible and enthusiastic.

The first Christians looked forward to the second coming of Christ in glory. His first coming was in the hiddenness of Mary's womb and the frailty of human mortality. His return was promised in unambiguous glory, as the judge of the living and the dead. History will then take a new and remarkable turn, for with the death of death, the extinction of our sinful nature, and the extermination of evil forces, time itself will be left behind in the glories of a love-saturated eternity.

To pray for God's kingdom to come is therefore a prayer in two time zones. For the present, we seek the immediate strengthening and advance of the kingdom. For the future, we pray for its completion. The Old Testament prophets demonstrate consistently the way in which the future should shape the present: we need to ready ourselves for the future, living lives of preparedness; and we need to live in the present in the light of eternal priorities. There is certainly nothing wrong with enjoying this life – whether pleasures or beauty, loving relationships or success – because the God who created life on earth concluded that it was 'very good'. We do not measure true spirituality by a boredom, indifference or disapproval towards the pleasures of today. But the present in God's kingdom is shot through with anticipation of the future. Life takes on an extra dimension, so that the ultimate concerns of those who only live for today are relativised by the priorities of eternal life. We may love sport, art, or making money, but we will not allow such pleasures to become our consuming passion. Our perspective on life is built on the prospect of Christ's return and the unfolding of eternity in the fullness of his love.

There is a fourth zone of the kingdom of God. While there are three zones within time, the fullness of the eternal kingdom is found beyond time, in the glory of heaven. Jesus invites us to embrace this eternal reality as we pray 'on earth as it is in heaven'. What we long for on earth is already accomplished in heaven, where sin and death have no right of access. We are therefore praying for the actualisation in time of eternal, heavenly realities. The present continuous existence of heaven connects with earth supremely in the first and second comings of Christ. Between his comings, in every act of righteousness and kindness, every moment of responsiveness to the God who speaks by Word and Spirit, every expression of repentance, worship and faith, an interconnection is established between heaven and earth.

When we pray for God's kingdom to come, we are not praying for something to be created out of nothing, in the manner of the original creation of the cosmos. Rather, we pray for a love that already finds perfect expression, in the timeless present of eternity, to pervade our daily existence, and to speed the day when death and sickness, sorrow and sin shall be no more. What is enjoyed in heaven, without beginning or end, will eventually arise even here, in the space-time continuum of earthly existence. The prayer of Jesus will find its ultimate fulfilment in his promised return.

Personal reflection

Is future hope an integral part of your daily perspective on life?

6

Yours is the kingdom

Modern Bible translations include only as a footnote the great doxology with which the Lord's Prayer ends. Although familiar to countless Christians through repetition of the traditional form of the prayer, it only appears in later manuscripts. It is best interpreted, therefore, as an early Church interpretative supplement to the words of Jesus. The words flow very naturally from the rest of the prayer, and ensure that the prayer is completed with an upbeat expression of praise.

The resounding declaration, 'Yours is the kingdom', reaffirms that at the heart of all kingdom talk is not a concept or a manifesto but the living God. The kingdom is therefore profoundly personal, as a kingdom of love. It has an uncontestable ruler, so that no human leader should dare claim control of the kingdom's agenda. And it has an irresistible force, since what God has spoken is guaranteed to advance towards its ultimate and eternal fulfilment.

'Power' affirms God's capacity to enact his words. The source of all life is sure to accomplish the fullness of his reconciling purposes. The word can also be translated as 'authority'. The two concepts are very close, but authority emphasises that there is no ultimate duality in the cosmos. Evil is a reality, but it is a strictly subordinate rather than an equal and opposite force to God. 'Authority' also recalls the Great Commission, where the risen Christ explains that he has been given all authority. The New Testament pattern of praying, baptising and exercising deliverance ministry 'in Jesus' name' reflects the early Christian confidence that the Son has been granted the delegated authority of the Father over every aspect of human existence.

'Glory' has a three-stranded meaning within the Bible. First, it acknowledges that God is fully deserving of all our praise, and more. He is the glorious one, both in his character and in the extravagance of his grace, for he has provided not only life itself, but also the free gift of salvation for a race that had sunk into selfishness, spiritual indifference or even hostility to God and his ways. Second, from the time of the Exodus the 'glory of the Lord' had been manifest among the Jews at decisive moments. The greatest, indeed the definitive, revelation of God is found in Christ Jesus, for in him all the fullness of the deity is found in bodily form. The glory of Christ's exemplary life is nothing less than the manifest glory of the living God. Third, Jesus gave a new twist to the understanding of 'glory', by referring to his impending crucifixion as his glorification. Until that time, the 'glory of the Lord' was understood to mean a demonstration of his majesty and might. For Jesus, it was in the extravagance of servanthood, suffering even to death for the sake of others, that the glory of God was most fully expressed. The self-humbling and self-abasement of God, stooping to embrace even mortality in order to rescue the lost: this is the ultimate expression of his glory.

The tone of this addition to Jesus' prayer is resounding praise. Intercession and adoration are never far apart in biblical praying. The requests of Jesus' prayer are underlined with confidence in this joyful expression of confident trust in the provision of the living God. Once again prayer opens up the connections between the present and the future: for one day every knee will bow and declare the glory of the risen Christ. And once again prayer interconnects earthly existence and the timeless moment of eternity. Just as heaven is filled with the praise of God, this closing doxology invites us to discover heaven's echo on earth. Our praise may be a pale reflection of the angelic hosts, but God is no less deserving of our praise.

The requests of Jesus' prayer can therefore be expressed with quiet confidence, safe in the knowledge of the power and glory of our Father God. In the ebb and flow of praise and prayer, our faith is strengthened for daily living, and our hearts quicken with longing for the praise of the kingdom of heaven, for which the grandest heights of worship in this life are no more than an early rehearsal. The best, for every citizen of the kingdom of God, is always yet to come.

Prayer response

Use the concluding doxology of the Lord's Prayer, whether said or sung and perhaps repeated several times, as your personal echo of heaven's eternal song of praise.

7

Bible Meditation

ISAIAH 61:1–4

Isaiah sums up the priorities of the kingdom of God in the scripture that Jesus used to introduce his own public ministry. This was the passage that he chose to read in the synagogue in what has become known as the Nazareth Manifesto (Luke 4:16–21). When he finished reading from the scroll, Jesus sat down to indicate that he was about to teach from the passage, and at once made an astonishing claim: 'Today this scripture is fulfilled in your hearing.'

Isaiah 61 begins by affirming the initiative of God. It is only because the Spirit of the Lord is upon the servant, anointing him to the task, that he can be used as the great advancer of the kingdom. There is no place here for complacency, arrogance, or self-assertion, but rather dependence upon the resources of God. Only by God's power can his kingdom advance.

What follows is a series of dramatic reversals:

- the good news is preached to the poor, who are so often excluded from the privileges of human religion;
- the broken-hearted are given healing, the captives freedom, and prisoners release from darkness;
- those who grieve are given a threefold exchange: a crown of beauty

for ashes, the oil of gladness instead of mourning, a garment of praise in place of despair.

These images have a literal and a metaphorical force: God promises both a transformation of society, and also a transformation of our inner life. Slaves will find their shackles severed, even as those walking in an inner bondage and darkness can know an emotional and spiritual liberation. There is no need to choose between the inward and societal implications: they are both integral to the rescuing purposes of God. The social gospel Christian, who loses the dimension of personal, saving faith, and the pietistic Christian, who loses the socio-political implications of God's kingdom, both end up with a truncated gospel, failing to recognise the all-embracing wholeness of biblical teaching on the kingdom of God.

The final contrast in the passage is between ruins and forests. The cities of Israel have literally been destroyed by invading armies, and will be rebuilt. But the most striking expression of new hope is that God's people – scattered, weak and small in number – will be known as 'oaks of righteousness'. Just as a country estate can enjoy a cultivated woodland, God will establish his people as a planting, majestic and enduring, for 'the display of his splendour'.

This remarkable agenda for the kingdom provides some extraordinarily life-enriching prospects:

- to affirm our dependence upon the anointing presence of God's Spirit;
- to retain a fiercely optimistic hope that God can reverse the most desperate of circumstances;
- to embrace our responsibility to work and pray for God's righteousness to find ever fuller expression in our society and around the world;
- to open our hearts to God for inner transformation in the superabundant hope and life of the kingdom.

Prayer

O God of the kingdom of righteousness, deepen my inner liberation and renewal in your eternal love, and quicken me to a life of service according to the priorities of your kingdom. Bring more of your kingdom into my life and more of your kingdom through my life. In the name of Jesus Christ, the kingdom bringer. Amen.

DEVOTIONAL POEMS

Hear me, O God!
A broken heart
Is my best part:
Use still thy rod
That I may prove
Therein thy love.

If thou hadst not
Been stern to me,
But left me free,
I had forgot
Myself and thee.

For sin's so sweet,
As minds ill bent
Rarely repent,
Until they meet
Their punishment.

Who more can crave
Than thou hast done?
That gav'st a Son,
To free a slave,
First made of naught;
With all since bought.

Sin, Death and Hell
His glorious Name
Quite overcame,
Yet I rebel,
And slight the same.

But I'll come in,
Before my loss
Me farther toss,
As sure to win
Under his cross.

Ben Jonson, 1573–1637

TO HEAVEN

Good and great God, can I not think of thee,
But it must straight my melancholy be?
Is it interpreted in me disease
That, laden with my sins, I seek for ease?
Oh, be thou witness, that the reins dost know
And hearts of all, if I be sad for show;
And judge me after, if I dare pretend
To aught but grace, or aim at other end.
As thou art all, so be thou all to me,
First, midst, and last; converted one and three;
My faith, my hope, my love; and in this state,
My judge, my witness, and my advocate.
Where have I been this while exiled from thee?
And whither rapt, now thou but stoop'st to me?
Dwell, dwell here still: Oh, being everywhere,
How can I doubt to find thee ever here?
I know my state, both full of shame and scorn,
Conceived in sin, and unto labour born,
Standing with fear, and must with horror fall,

And destined unto judgment, after all.
I feel my griefs too, and there scarce is ground
Upon my flesh to inflict another wound.
Yet dare I not complain, or wish for death
With holy Paul, lest it be thought the breath
Of discontent; or that these prayers be
For weariness of life, not love of thee.

Ben Jonson

THE SINNER'S SACRIFICE TO THE HOLY TRINITY

Oh holy, blessed, glorious Trinity
Of persons, still one God in unity,
The faithful man's believed mystery,
Help, help to lift

Myself up to thee, harrowed, torn and bruised
By sin and Satan; and my flesh misused,
As my heart lies in pieces, all confused,
Oh, take my gift.

All-gracious God, the sinner's sacrifice,
A broken heart thou wert not wont despise,
But 'bove the fat of rams, or bulls, to prize
An offering meet

For thy acceptance. Oh, behold me right,
And take compassion on my grievous plight.
What odour can be, than a heart contrite,
To thee more sweet?

Eternal Father, God who didst create
This all of nothing, gav'st it form and fate,
And breath'st into it life and light, with state
To worship thee;

Eternal God the Son, who not denied
To take our nature, becam'st man, and died
To pay our debts, upon thy cross, and cried
All's done in me;

Eternal Spirit, God from both proceeding,
Father and Son, the comforter in breeding
Pure thoughts in man; with fiery zeal them feeding
For acts of grace:

Increase those acts, O glorious Trinity
Of persons, still one God in unity,
Till I attain the longed-for mystery
Of seeing your face,

Beholding one in three, and three in one,
A Trinity, to shine in union;
The gladdest light dark man can think upon,
O grant it me!

Father, and Son, and Holy Ghost, you three
All co-eternal in your majesty,
Distinct in persons, yet in unity
One God to see,

My Maker, Saviour, and my Sanctifier,
To hear, to meditate, sweeten my desire
With grace, with love, with cherishing entire;
Oh, then how blest,

Among thy saints elected to abide,
And with thy angels placed side by side,
But in thy presence truly glorified,
Shall I there rest!

Ben Jonson

At the round earth's imagin'd corners, blow
Your trumpets, angels, and arise, arise
From death, you numberless infinities
Of souls, and to your scattered bodies go,
All whom the flood did, and fire shall o'erthrow,
All whom war, dearth, age, agues, tyrannies,
Despair, law, chance, hath slain, and you whose eyes,
Shall behold God, and never taste death's woe.
But let them sleep, Lord, and me mourn a space,
For, if above all these, my sins abound,
'Tis late to ask abundance of thy grace,
When we are there; here on this lowly ground,
Teach me how to repent; for that's as good
As if thou hadst seal'd my pardon, with thy blood.

John Donne

CHAPTER III

GIVE US TODAY OUR DAILY BREAD

Give us this day our daily bread

WHITSUNDAY

Listen sweet Dove unto my song,
And spread thy golden wings in me;
Hatching my tender heart so long,
Till it get wing, and fly away with thee.

Where is that fire which once descended
On thy Apostles? Thou didst then
Keep open house, richly attended,
Feasting all comers by twelve chosen men.

Such glorious gifts thou didst bestow,
That th'earth did like a heav'n appear;
The stars were coming down to know
If they might mend their wages, and serve here.

The sun, which once did shine alone,
Hung down his head, and wished for night,
When he beheld twelve suns for One
Going about the world, and giving light.

But since those pipes of gold, which brought
The cordial water to our ground,
Were cut and martyred by the fault
Of those, who did themselves through their side wound,

Thou shutt'st the door and keep'st within;
Scarce a good joy creeps through the chink:
And if the braves of conqu'ring sin
Did not excite thee, we should wholly sink.

Lord, though we change, thou art the same;
The same sweet God of love and light:
Restore this day, for thy great name,
Unto his ancient and miraculous right.

George Herbert

1

Give us today

Jesus moves effortlessly from prayers that embrace the destiny of the cosmos to our concern with practical, daily needs. To some it can seem almost impertinent to trouble God with the trivia of life. Surely he has far too many important concerns to be bothered with the details of our daily existence. How can a transcendent God, whose worship absorbs the whole company of heaven, have any interest in our daily diet? Jesus' prayer, however, confidently asserts divine involvement in our everyday lives. The Lord of the cosmos lacks neither the capacity nor the concern to attend to our daily needs: the next meal of mortal men and women really does matter to our loving heavenly Father.

For the rich in the West today, this way of praying can seem not so much inappropriate as irrelevant. The fridge and freezer can usually provide us with plenty, and if our stocks have run low, a twenty-four-hour supermarket is only a short car drive away. Although some have retained the habit of giving thanks for their meals, as a society we have little sense of dependence upon the rains or the harvest. For those living in Britain, the rains have never been known to fail in living memory – especially during the first week of the Wimbledon Lawn Tennis Championships! The privileges of the developed world may seem to have made Jesus' request superfluous, something to which we may still deign to give lip service but which no longer carries any real sense of priority.

The same request would sound very different within a traditional peasant community, dependent upon subsistence farming. If it fails to rain at the right time or rains heavily at the wrong time, the crops will fail and a full-scale famine may threaten. Similarly for the fishermen of Galilee, when their existence was from hand to mouth, the success of the next fishing trip was always critical. Their prayer for daily provision would have an unmistakable and customary edge of urgency.

The Christian faith has always been plagued by super-spiritual excesses. Some have tried to suggest that the truly spiritual ascend to a higher plane of indifference to bodily existence, becoming oblivious to material concerns and unsullied by such experiences as taking pleasure in a good meal. By making his prayer explicitly address the practical need for a full stomach, Jesus repudiates any otherworldly approach to prayer. Here is a God who is genuinely concerned for a full stomach, if not for the detailed calculations of our daily calorie intake. There is no room for a false spirituality that wants to create a rigid divide between the so-called 'important' spiritual existence and the 'unimportant' life of the body. As C. S. Lewis once observed, 'God likes matter, he invented it.'

Through this request for daily food, Jesus invites us to develop an approach to prayer that embraces every aspect of life. He wants us to declare with confidence our Father's concern and direct involvement in the ordinariness of our everyday existence. There is nothing in our lives which is off limits when it comes to presenting requests to our Father in heaven. Whether we are preoccupied with work and money, health and housing or our children's education and development, Jesus encourages us to bring our personal needs before God. Our heavenly Father's dedicated involvement in our lives will even encompass every leisure pursuit that brings us pleasure and fulfilment, be it golf or gardening, cooking or cars. What matters to us matters also to God, because of his great love for every individual.

There is, of course, an important limit upon Jesus' permission in this respect. Just as some Christians mistakenly fear that it would be impertinent to bring their personal needs to God, others have no such qualms and offer up an ever-expanding catalogue of personal requests. The Lord's Prayer gives us permission to get personal with God, but also sets such needs in a broader context of prayer. Self-obsession invariably leads to a self-limited individual, unable to fulfil their potential and showing little interest in others. Those whose requests never reach beyond their own needs condemn themselves to a cramped and superficial grasp of prayer.

Jesus' phrase goes much further than giving us permission to pray about our meals and our other day-to-day concerns. Even as Jesus invites us to pray to God as Father, in a relationship of intimate love, he also reminds us to acknowledge our creaturely dependence upon the Lord of Creation. Those living close to nature are likely to have a greater sense of the precariousness of human existence: at any moment life can be forfeit to disease or injury, in any year the rains may not come and the crops may fail. In the modern West, we run the risk of taking for granted not only our daily food, but even life itself. We become so cocksure, so self-assured, that a self-satisfied arrogance begins to corrupt our attitude even towards God. The Pharisee in Jesus' parable about humble prayer demonstrates the inability of the self-made man to pray with the true humility of creaturely dependence. He is too full of himself to receive much from God, too pleased with himself to give much honour to the giver and sustainer of life. Jesus' prayer is a timely reminder that life itself, as much as the sunrise and the seasonal cycle, is a gift of God.

For those in the developed world this declaration of creaturely dependence is particularly important, for it emphasises that genuine humility before the Creator is a vital ingredient of healthy prayer. When we address God as Father we are exalted in the immensity of his love, but when we make our request for daily bread – even when the fridge is full – we make a necessary acknowledgment of our smallness, vulnerability and dependence upon the transcendent Creator. No matter how great our personal wealth and success, our daily meals – from the lightest snack to the grandest banquet – and even life itself, are best enjoyed not as ours by right or achievement but rather as generous gifts of God.

Personal reflection

Have you begun to take the gift of life for granted, losing the vital awareness of creaturely dependence?

2

Give us bread

The smell of freshly baked bread is irresistible. It has been claimed that some supermarkets buy a chemical compound – essence of baked bread – and pump it through the store in order to increase sales. The smell makes us happy, and happy shoppers linger longer and so spend more. Jesus' prayer for daily food is specific. He calls us to pray not for the dish of the day or an à la carte menu, but specifically for bread. In the mid-nineteenth century, the poor in Europe would still sometimes bake a large loaf that would see them through the week. Anything more was a privilege and an extra. It is for bread as a staple food that we are invited to pray. That is, it is a daily loaf, not cakes and croissants, that Jesus would have us request. You might say that Irish Christians, in the spirit of Jesus' words, can pray for daily potatoes. Elsewhere in the world, Jesus' bread becomes an invitation to pray for daily pasta, noodles or rice.

Sophisticated palates can lose the pleasure in simple things. In the last few years coffee shops have been booming in Britain. The question is no longer 'with or without milk?' or 'cappuccino or espresso?' Trendy customers now have to be able to tell their Latte from their Leche and know what it means to ask for an extra shot. Although one of the instant coffee manufacturers has tried to hit back with a cafe serving only instant coffee, the writing may be on the wall for the cheaper substitute. Once a nation becomes accustomed to the taste of the real thing, there is no going back.

A generation ago in Britain, many poorer households made an appetising and inexpensive meal from bread and dripping. Today dripping (the congealed drips of fat from roast meat) would be shunned as a heart attack waiting to happen. The traditional white loaf has been replaced by countless options in the supermarkets, from cholla to pitta, from bagels to brioche. Faced with such delicious proliferation, the ordinary sliced loaf has been downwardly mobile for a generation. It has gone from the staple food to 'just bread', a mere filler to be consumed but hardly noticed or savoured.

The steadily rising standard of living among post-war generations can lead to a jaded palate. Not just literally, in terms of our attitude to food, but more broadly, we can become addicted to the new, constantly seeking something more – a more exotic holiday, a more luxurious car. We have become a society that finds it increasingly difficult to return to the pleasures of yesterday.

For some people the acquisition of new things is more important than the pleasure they bring. I remember a wealthy businessman showing me his new hi-fi system. The quality was sensational. In fact it was so good that the precision could only be fully appreciated from the technical data, for it transcended the capacity of the human ear. He asked me what I thought of it, and I enthused that it looked great and sounded superb. He looked relieved, and then explained, 'I needed someone else to tell me because I am partially deaf.' The pleasure, it seemed, was more in conspicuous consumption rather than enjoyment of the music.

The prayer for daily bread is an invitation not to lose sight of the small pleasures. We need to retain a sense of wonder and appreciation when we are faced with a bird singing, a rose in bloom, or a child's first step. When we remain truly appreciative of the little things of life, we cultivate a generous spirit that allows us to be thankful and encouraging towards other people and grateful towards God.

When I next take a bread roll or a single slice of bread, I want to enjoy it, not dismiss it out of hand as mere everyday bread. And as I savour its wholesomeness, I want to be thankful to the living God who has once again responded generously to my repetition of the prayer of Jesus.

Personal reflection

Could you be losing sight of appreciation for the small pleasures of life? Renew your thankfulness to God in the details of your everyday world.

3

Bread for the day

'Daily bread' recalls the manna of the Exodus (Exod. 16). The word 'manna' means 'what is it?' – which was the Israelites' first reaction to the new food. In the early morning, as the dew evaporated, thin white flakes resembling frost appeared on the ground. They gathered about two litres per person and found they could bake it or boil it. Moses described it as 'the bread the LORD has given you to eat'.

Daily manna was provided in the wilderness for the Israelites to scoop up and consume. It was naturally tempting to collect as much as possible, hoarding food in case of future shortages, or even as a means of making some extra income – a kind of black market in manna. However, manna had a short shelf life. The day of its supply proved also to be its sell-by date. Even as soon as the next morning, any surplus was full of maggots and smelt foul. The only exception was the Friday manna, which kept throughout Saturday so that they could observe the Sabbath without interruption. Those who went out for more manna on Saturdays were disappointed: none could ever be found. Six days of manna were sufficient for seven days of nourishment, even as six days of work are sufficient for seven days of life.

To pray for daily bread is therefore to identify with the Jews in the Exodus. It expresses a critical dependence upon God for daily provision. It also reminds us that God's provision is sufficiency, not surplus. The prayer is for bread, because Jesus wants to assure us of God's concern for our daily needs, rather than guaranteeing that God will meet our most grandiose desires. This is no prayer for a lifestyle of caviar and Ferraris, but a universal prayer for enough. That certainly does not make a meal of more than bread a sin, or food in the freezer a betrayal of true spirituality! But it does mean that we should keep things in due proportion: our life is worth far more than food, drink and material possessions, and such things should never be allowed to become our ultimate concern.

Eating disorders, often associated with low self-esteem, have been steadily rising across the West, and have recently begun to show a new increase among teenage boys, even though the great majority of sufferers are still women. Some people turn an excessive appetite into a demi-god, compulsively gorging themselves at every opportunity. The Bible warns that an obsession with food can become self-destructive, and so gluttony is associated with idolatry. For others the rigorous exclusion of food, whether through constant dieting, self-induced vomiting, or the self-deprivation of anorexia nervosa, is equally compulsive. Many have become inwardly convinced that every pair of scales decrees that they are grossly disfigured by corpulence. Looking into a mirror, their eyes see skin and bones, but their mind sees repulsive slabs of fat.

The prayer for daily bread marks the fine balance between extremes. For the glutton, it is a reminder of the need for self-restraint, since God's concern is for sufficient food, not tables heaving under a gargantuan excess. For the underweight, it is an invitation to eat at least a little more, confident that God's best purposes include a liberation from the torture of endlessly seeking to become even thinner.

For most of us, unlike the Israelites in Moses' day, supernatural bread tends not to be deposited on a regular basis in our back gardens. We have to work for it. Work in the Old Testament is viewed in two ways. On the one hand, it is a gift of God in creation. To work is an expression of being made in the image of an active God. Productive work enhances our well-being, our sense of purpose and achievement. Creating a fair profit is a reflection of the creativity of a God who creates out of nothing. At the same time, this gift of God has been distorted by the curse of the fall. As a result, work has come to be experienced as dehumanising drudgery, often marked more by sweat and toil than by fulfilment. The general tendency of the Western Church to polarise life into the sacred and secular has resulted in the devaluation of work, as something that simply has to be done in order to release us for the more interesting and significant spiritual aspects of life. But to pray for daily bread is to pray for our work as well as our food, with a confidence that God goes with us into our workplace and is our protector and provider in every aspect of life.

Jesus' parables paint a graphic picture of a society in which many working men would hang around in the town square, waiting for someone to take them on as casual labour for the day. For them, quite literally, the prayer for daily bread was a prayer for a single day's work and pay. In exactly the same way, Jesus' prayer urges us to involve God in the world of work and to consider our Father in heaven as our primary Careers' Adviser and Personnel Director. God is really interested in our next career move, an overdue and well-deserved pay rise, the difficult person at the office, or the ethical dilemma we are facing.

Daily bread also speaks of the importance of living one day at a time. Jesus made no objection to planning ahead, but he did warn his followers not to get sucked into worrying about the future. Each day, he explained, has enough cares of its own. For those inclined not so much to plan ahead as to worry ahead, clogging up the present with dire prospects for the future that rarely, if ever, happen in practice, Jesus anchors us in the present. He calls us to stay focused and to live as we pray. As we renew our request for bread for today, we discipline ourselves not to become over-anxious about next year's culinary prospects.

Some parents concentrate their worries on their children: from the first step to the first girlfriend, the first trip on a train alone to the first late-night party, parenthood can feel like walking through a minefield of anxieties. As Jean, the mother of a twenty-something, shrugged her shoulders and explained to me, 'The trouble is, you never stop being their mum, and there's always something new to worry about.' The prayer for daily bread is a prayer for the family – for provision and also for protection. It can be prayed with urgency for a wayward adolescent or someone in a mid-life crisis, for an aged parent or someone you love who has a debilitating or life-threatening condition. To pray for daily bread is to pray one day at a time – strength for the next twenty-four hours.

Food, like sleep, is one of life's necessities. Although we may skip meals safely from time to time, if we go without food for a longer period, our life quickly becomes at risk. Prayer has rarely been seen in such terms. Christians in the modern West live increasingly secularised lives. There seems to be no time to pray, as our schedules become fuller with every passing year. More fundamentally, we live in a society that operates most of the time without reference to God. Spirituality has been squeezed to the margins of life: an optional extra for those with a particular interest in such things, with no more claim to be one of life's essentials than stamp collecting or ballroom dancing. Daytime TV has elevated 'keep fit' as one of life's necessities, but spirituality still languishes in the shadows. Apparently you have to be unusually religious, traditionalist or a little eccentric to make the effort to pray.

By inviting us to pray for daily bread, Jesus is making a statement about regular prayer and not just regular food. The only way to take the request for daily food seriously is to revisit the prayer every day. Jesus' prayer freely acknowledges that we need enough food, and that God is interested in such mundane and practical concerns. At the same time Jesus clearly intimates that to enjoy a healthy life we also need to ensure that we protect space for personal prayer.

Personal reflection

For what need or concern are you in need of 'bread for today'?

4

Bread for others

In urban settings, many no longer know their neighbours: in some areas people are always moving house, in others people are instinctively wary of strangers. With families scattered and neighbours unknown, community entertainment and the local pub have been replaced by the TV and a six-pack from the supermarket. Behind closed doors we live isolated lives. Recent surveys have revealed a startling, but logically inevitable, consequence of this increasingly individualised existence: among those in their twenties there is little remaining sense of responsibility towards others. We earn our own money and live our own lives, and it is up to others to do the same. A lottery ticket is much more appealing as an impulse purchase than a donation to charity. Cocooned in privacy, we do our own thing.

The Lord's Prayer confronts Western individualism head-on. Even as the prayer begins by acknowledging the privileged access to God the Father that is available to all believers – not just 'my' but 'our' Father – when we pray for bread it is also in the first person plural. We cannot pray for 'our bread' and remain indifferent to the poor, unemployed or elderly in our church. We cannot pray collectively but consume individually, tucking into a hearty meal sublimely indifferent to those who are less well off. Jesus' words compel us to embrace collective responsibility. We are indeed our brother's keeper, for we pray for *his* daily bread as well as our own.

The early Church in Jerusalem embraced a communal responsibility that is quite alien to the customary practice of most Western churches (Acts 2:44–5; 4:32–5). Luke reports that those with wealth were more than willing to hand some over for the benefit of the poor. No one, he explains, considered any of their possessions their own, and so they shared everything that they had, with the result that no one among them was left in need.

This was no compulsory confiscation of personal wealth into a centralised account run by neo-Marxist apostles. There was no suggestion that wealth was wrong or property theft. Luke speaks of individual possessions, which means they retained a sense of ownership, but they sat lightly to it, gladly sharing what they enjoyed or even selling it outright in order to hand over money for distribution among the poor. When the Jerusalem church prayed for '*our* daily bread', the rich unmistakably faced up to their responsibilities towards the poor.

Later Paul organised an offering among the churches he had planted for the Jerusalem church, which had fallen upon hard times. The early Christians quickly grasped that the implications of the gospel could not be restricted to their own local church or ethnic grouping. And so across the political boundaries, local churches gave willingly and generously to their needy brothers and sisters, even though they lived far away. In particular Paul commended the Macedonian churches to the Corinthians, who had been quick to make a verbal offer of help but slow in providing actual donations (2 Cor. 8–9).

The Macedonians had experienced a severe time of testing and were suffering extreme poverty. It seems that Paul may have felt obliged to exempt them from his general appeal for the Jerusalem offering, since their circumstances were so grim. However, when they got to hear about it, they urgently pleaded for the privilege of sharing in this service. And when they gave, they handed over not merely as much as they were able but went far beyond what could reasonably have been expected, extravagant in their generosity. When the Macedonian believers, even in their poverty, prayed for 'our' daily bread, they recognised and gave practical expression to their solidarity with impoverished believers in other parts of the world.

There is no wriggling out of the logic of our responsibility. When we pray for bread for the poor, we implicate ourselves in our praying, and so we need to make our resources available as a means by which God can answer the prayers of our lips. The prayer that binds us together with others in our common faith binds our wealth to their poverty, our food stocks to their empty stomachs. The Lord's Prayer leaves no place for Western silos filled to the brim with surplus grain, nor Western banks taking more in interest payments from developing nations than our governments provide in aid. The Old and New Testament command to love our neighbours as ourselves, the repeated cry of the Old Testament prophets for God's justice for the poor, and the prayer for one another's daily bread all lead to the same conclusion. Biblical religion is immensely practical and compassionate: we must share our food and wealth with those for whom we pray.

Some Christians devote a great deal of energy to praying about their own prosperity. In truth, compared to the rest of the world and previous generations, almost everyone in the Western world enjoys a remarkably high standard of material well–being. Our lifestyle is a privilege, but it should not be our preoccupation. The prayer for daily bread certainly carries no implication that believers are required to repudiate all privileges of material prosperity. But I would rather pray for bread for the starving than for caviar for myself. And then I must do something, however modest and apparently insignificant, in a practical response to their needs.

Personal reflection

What practical steps could you take to share your prosperity with others?

5

Bread for the coming day

Some people are destined for the mornings. They wake up with a smile, moving instantaneously from deep sleep to hyper-activity. Their ideal business meeting requires high-octane negotiation over the breakfast bacon. In the evenings, the pattern is reversed, for if they are kept up beyond a certain time their brain and body spontaneously de-activate and they slump into sudden somnolence. Others believe that waking up is an activity best approached with due care and attention. Like an animal arousing from hibernation, it takes time for full bodily function to be restored. In the worst cases, the anaesthetic of sleep does not fully wear off until the mid-morning coffee break. Their ideal time for creative thinking is around midnight, when the brain's juices really begin to flow.

In a commendable desire to 'pray properly' young Christians sometimes try to emulate the spiritual superstar of their denomination or stream. 'If it was good enough for John and Charles to start praying at 4 a.m.,' they declare, 'it must be good enough for me.' Such zeal conspicuously fails to take account of a number of variables. In a world without electric lights, people often went to bed at times now reserved for young children and the elderly. Similarly, waking hours were much more closely tied to the available hours of daylight. What is more, if the hero is a morning person and the ardent disciple is a night owl, the emulation may be well-intended but is likely to be short lived.

Fortunately for all of us, the New Testament consistently avoids decreeing set hours for prayer, whether early or late. The Lord's Prayer itself works equally well at both ends of the day. Prayed in the morning, we request bread for the same day. Prayed in the evening, we request bread for the next. The cares of the day are handed over to our Father in heaven at the beginning of the day. At night we consign to the Father's care the concerns of tomorrow, so that we might sleep in peace.

Bread for the coming day also has a more developed, eschatological meaning. Anticipating persecution among the followers of the crucified, we pray for God's provision even to the end of this age. The One who keeps faith with his beloved servants in the daily necessities of life will not fail us in the hour of arrest or martyrdom.

Between tomorrow's bread and the end of time is 'bread for the coming day' when we have to learn to stare death in the face. Many people have no emotional grasp of their own mortality until mid-life. Some only begin to face the reality of their own death when coming to terms with the death of one of their parents. Traffic accidents are so high among the young precisely because they tend to consider themselves immune in the face of danger. For many, a terminal diagnosis is met at first not with fear but denial: 'It seems like a dream, or rather a nightmare; something that could not possibly be happening to me.'

Bread for the time of dying is a remarkable provision. I remember sitting with Joan as she waited to die. There were no treatments left in the medical arsenal save painkilling cocktails, as potent as the doctors could risk. The skin had shrunk taut on her skeletal body. Her hands were bony and frail beyond her years. And yet a quiet dignity had come upon her. There was such a peace in her presence that those who visited her, seeking to provide some comfort, were comforted by her remarkable composure. Even as her lingering body gradually wasted away, she was nourished inwardly by her Father in heaven. Always she found there was bread for the day.

Henry's death was very different. The diagnosis came very late. Like lions upon their prey, the deathly tumours tore into his body with terrible speed. After a few days in hospital, he knew he was dying, even though no word had been said. 'Rob,' he cried, 'I'm just not ready to die!' There are times to pray for healing and times to prepare for death. His whole expression told me he knew that death was drawing close, even as he declared his unpreparedness. There was only time for a brief prayer: 'Lord Jesus, in your mercy, grant your beloved servant bread for the coming day.' By the next morning, Henry had need of daily bread no more.

What is true for persecution, martyrdom and imminent death is also true for other times of great pressure. When James's office became ensnared in a tumultuous power struggle, and redundancies were sure to follow, 'bread for the coming day' became the request that sustained him and expressed his deepest need. When Elsa experienced the half-life of chemotherapy, assailed by the drugs that were combatting her deadly cancer, she was unsure at times whether she felt more dead or alive. Later, when every trace of cancer had been obliterated, she too revealed that one prayer had been her constant companion – bread for the coming day.

Prayer response

If you know someone who may be close to death, pray that they will have 'bread for the coming day'.

6

The bread of life

When Jesus established the unique meal of the Christian Church, he adapted a Jewish meal that was at once very special and yet rooted in the everyday. Very special, because it was the Passover, the meal celebrating the events that had forever shaped Jewish history and identity. This was the meal of their liberation from slavery in Egypt, of a generation's wandering in the desert, and their final entry into the Promised Land. It was the meal of the covenant, in which God became their God and they became his people. No Jewish family ate the meal without remembering and reflecting in considerable detail upon the events of the original Passover, in which the blood of the sacrificial lamb, daubed upon the doorposts, exempted Israelite families from the fearful visitation by the angel of death upon the oldest sons in Egypt.

The specific elements upon which Jesus concentrated were, of course, the bread and the wine. He thus removed from an elaborate ceremonial meal the two elements that made up the standard meal of a middle Eastern peasant – the bread that nourished and the wine which was certainly no luxury item, but much safer to drink than untreated water.

Jesus' meal therefore points in three directions. First, it is the Christian equivalent of the Passover meal, a symbolic feast that celebrates our liberation from slavery and entry into the life of promise, rescued by the living God. Second, it is the meal of everyday. No Palestinian peasant would have been too poor to afford a meal so inexpensive and simple: bread and wine is a meal as rudimentary as anyone could conceive. Third, it is the meal that points to Christ and his cross: his is the atoning sacrifice as the once-for-all Passover sacrifice, the Lamb of God who takes away the sins of the world.

For the Jews, the Passover meal is consumed as a family, children and grandparents joining together in the feast. The saving acts of God in human history find domestic expression, for the God of all generations is also the God of the family. But the peasant meal of bread and wine, lacking all the trimmings of the full Passover, was a meal consumed by tens of thousands every day. Jesus therefore retains the symbolism of the Passover, giving it new meaning and fulfilment in his own consummate self-sacrifice. But he also removes the meal of the Church from the setting of a special annual festival, and roots it in the everyday.

Communion has three tenses. We remember what has been accomplished once for all at the cross – Christ has died. We acknowledge that, as a result of being raised into resurrection life, we live under the present-day rule of the Saviour – Christ is risen. And we anticipate the great and glorious end of history, when God's redemptive purposes are fulfilled – Christ will come again. It is certainly true to say that this is a memorial feast. Without the cross and resurrection, the meal would have no meaning or value at all. But it is more than a celebration of the past, for it is also a meal of expectancy concerning Christ's return, and at the same time a means of present-day encounter with Christ. Some Christians have wanted to reduce the meal to a merely symbolic experience, rooted in the past. Others have suggested that the bread and wine undergo a literal change into Christ's body and blood. The middle path has always seemed to me to be the most convincing: even as we are nourished physically by the bread and wine that we consume, by the Holy

Spirit we have a simultaneous opportunity to feed on Christ by faith in our hearts.

Although most churches have preferred to restrict their understanding of the communion meal to a public celebration, presided over by an ordained minister, it has always seemed to me that Jesus' approach allows for a greater degree of flexibility. To be sure, the meal finds fullest expression when we eat in fellowship together. And yet surely there is a sense in which every bite of bread, every mouthful of wine, becomes charged with a supernatural level of meaning. We eat in remembrance not merely in the formal and public eucharistic feast, but on every occasion when we bite into our daily bread. In the midst of a peasant meal we taste the presence and saving power of Jesus Christ. Every taste of red wine reminds us anew that we are saved and kept by the shed blood of the Lamb, safe in the covenant that was sealed in his blood. This is not to diminish the value of sharing regularly in communion together. But every simple meal becomes a small sign of our union with Christ and glorious dependence upon his cross. The ordinary is overlaid with the supernatural. 'Daily bread' speaks not only of bodily sustenance but also of a daily feeding upon Jesus, the bread of life.

The meal that speaks of the past and present speaks also of the future. Jesus explained that he would not 'drink again of the fruit of the vine until the kingdom of God comes' (Luke 22:18). Even as we anticipate the return of Christ in glory, we also anticipate a great and glorious meal that will usher in this new era: the wedding banquet of the Lamb. 'Bread for the coming day' therefore speaks not only of carbohydrate for tomorrow and God's strengthening in our times of greatest need. It also looks forward to the greatest meal of all, when the human race comes into its divinely appointed destiny – life in all its fullness in the eternal kingdom of love.

A simple mouthful of lunchtime bread is given many layers of new and rich meaning. We eat with thankfulness that God has been our provider. We eat trusting God to supply our every need, casting our cares upon a practical God who is compassionate and concerned for our daily and bodily needs. We eat with responsibility for those on the brink of starvation. We eat in memory of the astonishing miracle of the cross of Christ, where God died for his enemies. We eat with confidence in the risen Christ and feed on him in our hearts. We eat in expectation of Christ's return, and the banquet that will celebrate the end of time. Time and eternity pervade as simple and homely an act as eating a slice of bread. When we pray for bread, we request not merely physical sustenance, but we choose to see the simplest acts of daily living shot through with eternal significance. Those who have begun to see these deeper meanings are no longer able to eat a single crust without wonder and thanksgiving.

Personal reflection

If you eat some bread today, make every effort to consume it with wonder and thanksgiving.

7

Bible Meditation

EXODUS 16

Before the manna was provided, the Jews were grumbling. In fact they made a profession of complaints, since nothing was more frequently heard from their lips. Even though they had just been miraculously liberated from slavery in Egypt, they were already declaring that they had been better off in their old life. Even so, we can become addicted to negativity, so that every conversation becomes a litany of complaints. The unguarded tongue has the capacity to obliterate thankfulness and extinguish hope.

Even as Jesus invited us to pray for daily bread, God's provision for the Jews during the Exodus was utterly reliable. No day came without fresh manna to harvest. There was even a double portion to be gathered on Fridays, so that there was no need to work for food on the Sabbath. Those who attempted to stockpile manna greedily found constant frustration: by the next morning the surplus was invariably filled with maggots and had a foul odour.

This ancient story speaks in very practical ways to several preoccupations that can become obsessive and even destructive in our lives.

- Those inclined to worry need to learn to trust God one day at a time, not amassing anxieties about future problems that may never arise.
- Workaholics need to learn to switch off from their responsibilities one day a week – six days are enough for anyone to work (five days are even better!).
- Those constantly attempting to obtain more wealth and material goods for themselves need to learn the biblical virtue of concern for others – their daily bread is more important than our daily luxuries.

DEVOTIONAL POEMS

Nature that washed her hands in milk
and had forgot to dry them,
In stead of earth took snow and silk
At Love's request to try them,
If she a mistress could compose
To please Love's fancy out of those.

Her eyes he would should be of light,
A violet breath, and lips of jelly,
Her hair not black, nor over bright,
And of the softest down her belly,
As for her inside he'd have it
Only of wantonness and wit.

At Love's entreaty, such a one
Nature made, but with her beauty
She hath framed a heart of stone,
So as Love by ill destiny
Must die for her whom nature gave him
Because her darling would not save him.

But Time which nature doth despise,
And rudely gives her love the lie,
Makes hope a fool, and sorrow wise,

His hands doth neither wash, nor dry,
But being made of steel and rust,
Turns snow, and silk, and milk to dust.

The Light, the belly, lips and breath,
He dims, discolours, and destroys,
With those he feeds, but fills not death,
Which sometimes were the food of joys;
Yea Time doth dull each lively wit,
And dries all wantonness with it.

Oh cruel Time which takes in trust
Our youth, our joys and all we have,
And pays us but with age and dust,
Who in the dark and silent grave
When we have wandered all our ways
Shuts up the story of our days.

Sir Walter Ralegh, 1552–1618

These verses following were made by Sir Walter Ralegh the night before he died and left at the Gate house.

Even such is time which takes in trust
Our youth, our joys, and all we have,
And pays us but with age and dust:
Who in the dark and silent grave
When we have wandered all our ways
Shuts up the story of our days.
And from which earth and grave and dust
The Lord shall raise me up, I trust.

ON THE LIFE OF MAN

What is our life? A play of passion,
Our mirth the music of division,
Our mothers' wombs the tiring houses be,
Where we are dressed for this short Comedy,
Heaven the Judicious sharp spectator is,
That sits and marks still who doth act amiss,
Our graves that hide us from the searching Sun,
Are like drawn curtains when the play is done,
Thus march we playing to our latest rest,
Only we die in earnest, that's no jest.

Sir Walter Ralegh

Death be not proud, though some have called thee
Mighty and dreadful, for, thou art not so,
For, those, whom thou think'st, thou dost overthrow,
Die not, poor death, nor yet canst thou kill me;
From rest and sleep, which but thy pictures be,
Much pleasure, then from thee, much more must flow,
And soonest our best men with thee do go,
Rest of their bones, and souls' delivery.
Thou art slave to Fate, chance, kings, and desperate men,
And dost with poison, war, and sickness dwell,
And poppy or charms can make us sleep as well,
And better than thy stroke; why swell'st thou then?
One short sleep past, we wake eternally,
And death shall be no more. Death, thou shalt die.

John Donne

CHAPTER IV

FORGIVE US OUR SINS AS WE FORGIVE THOSE WHO SIN AGAINST US

And forgive us our trespasses,
as we forgive those who trespass against us

REDEMPTION

Having been tenant long to a rich Lord,
Not thriving, I resolved to be bold,
And make a suit unto him, to afford
A new small-rented lease, and cancel th'old.
In heaven at his manor I him sought:
They told me there, that he was lately gone
About some land, which he had dearly bought
Long since on earth, to take possession.
I straight returned, and knowing his great birth,
Sought him accordingly in great resorts;
In cities, theatres, gardens, parks, and courts:
At length I heard a ragged noise and mirth
Of thieves and murderers: there I him espied,
Who straight, 'Your suit is granted' said, and died.

George Herbert

1

Sinners all

By including an appeal for forgiveness in his prayer, Jesus' conviction is unmistakable: his followers will never outgrow the need to be forgiven by the Father. The need to pray for forgiveness is not restricted to the early days of faith. It is not something we outgrow. On the contrary, the testimony of those believers down the centuries with an impeccable reputation for godly living is that the more they sought to serve God, the more painfully aware they became of their own shortcomings.

John Stott once remarked that many churchgoers are quite prepared to describe themselves as 'miserable offenders', but if someone addressed us personally as a 'miserable offender' we would instinctively want to punch our accuser on the nose! It is perfectly possible to give lip service to being sinners, while conducting ourselves with an entirely misplaced air of spiritual superiority.

Spiritual familiarity can breed complacency. We become so accustomed to church activities that we cease to scrutinise ourselves by God's standards. If our church happily tolerates gossip, back-biting, party spirit, spitefulness or resentment, we are tempted to join in. At best, church can be a foretaste of heaven; at worst, a foretaste of hell.

Others become so attentive to the shortcomings of others that they no longer notice their own. They see themselves as part of God's spiritual elite, the crack troops of the kingdom. Confident that they have more or less arrived, they look down upon other believers, whether within the same church or in other churches in town. They examine intently the splinters in the eyes of others, oblivious to the plank in their own.

Still others are confused about the impact of conversion. Having prayed for forgiveness and a fresh start, they assume that the direct, automatic and immediate result of being born again is that sin is exterminated and can no longer have any place in their lives. Sadly, there is absolutely no evidence in Christian history that this actually happens. Sooner or later, the sinful nature rears its ugly head and prompts selfish motivation and actions. Those with false expectations of the gospel will promptly begin to doubt whether they have ever become a Christian disciple at all.

That is not to say that conversion has no impact at all. Paul argues that the sinful nature continues to exist, but we are no longer in its power. It fights its corner, and sometimes secures great success for selfishness. But its domination of our lives is no longer automatic. Although we can give in to its cravings, we can choose to resist in the power of Christ and with the help of the Holy Spirit, putting to death the misdeeds of the selfish nature, rather than giving in to its every urge.

The first qualification for conversion is not an exemplary life, but the stark recognition that we are sinners. This means something far more profound than acknowledging that we have sometimes done wrong. The problem at the heart of the human condition is not merely isolated sins, but sinfulness. That means an inbuilt bias to self-centredness, rather than loving our neighbour as ourselves, and to the religion of self, rather than loving God with our whole being.

Once again, the first person plural is extremely telling. Jesus does not invite us to acknowledge our sinfulness before the Father in private, one to one. Rather, he expects us to accept this description of ourselves in public. This means there is a solidarity in sinfulness, a remarkable equality in which we all stand upon the same ground.

Here is no privileged position for the long-standing Christian, the dedicated activist, or the person whose family have been a part of the church for generations. We freely acknowledge as we pray Jesus' prayer that, without exception, we are all in need of fresh forgiveness.

This solidarity means there is no place for snobbishness, no justification for looking down upon particular individuals or sins. When Mandy became pregnant her parents were devastated: her father was a church elder and immediately offered his resignation. The church said they wanted him to continue, because they still appreciated his leadership. Since Mandy had retained enough of her Christian principles to refuse an abortion, a quick fling became a premature initiation into parenthood. The boyfriend had no interest in such responsibilities and melted away. And so a local church was introduced to a new moral dilemma: their disapproval of sex outside marriage was unequivocal, but would they now begin to treat Mandy and her daughter as spiritual outcasts? Although Mandy had done wrong at first, her decision to keep the child was commendable and brave. And her daughter was completely innocent. Fortunately the church rose to the occasion, generously giving Mandy all the love and support that she would need as she walked the tough path of single parenthood.

The church is not meant to be an assembly of Pharisees, looking down upon a sinful world with pious superiority, reluctant to demean itself by engaging in any normal, social activity for fear of moral and spiritual contamination. Nothing could be further from the lifestyle of Jesus, who went out of his way to mix with social outcasts – leprosy sufferers, tax collectors, prostitutes and the poor – the kind of 'low-lifes' and 'untouchables' who were utterly despised by the renowned and respected religious leaders of his day. But where Jesus' nature was uniquely pure, the rest of us share a universal condition of sinfulness. The Church is not an exclusive gathering of the sinless and devout. Nor is communion a meal reserved for those registering 100 per cent on the holiness scale. Jesus' prayer is for sinners only, and so is his Church and his meal.

The fact that we all continue to ask for forgiveness does more than underline our essential equality in our common, sinful humanity. It also alerts us to the need for sensible precautions. The instinct to gossip, negativity and party spirit lies dormant in all of us. Like an unprotected box of fireworks suddenly igniting from a casually dropped cigarette end, we can so easily light the blue touchpaper of the sinful nature with unguarded remarks. Sparks are sure to fly, and people will probably get hurt.

Similarly, Christians are certainly not immune to sexual temptation, and so a sensible church needs to establish an appropriate code of conduct for everyone involved in pastoral care. This will minimise the possibilities of misunderstanding and the dangers of anything getting out of hand. Counselling rooms need some glass in the door: not enough for the client to feel under public scrutiny, but sufficient for everyone to feel protected. If cross-sex counselling is permitted at all, there should be a third person present wherever possible, of the same sex as the client. Where leaders conduct home visits, some kind of accountability is required, to ensure that no one is receiving excessive or inappropriate attention. Some guidelines should also be established concerning the appropriate kinds of touch, both cross-sex and same-sex. Such precautions may seem heavy handed and an intrusion upon the privileges of the pastoral relationship, but in recent years there have been too many sad examples of sexual misdemeanour by Christian leaders and counsellors for the old, more relaxed patterns of pastoral conduct still to be tenable and credible. In a society where sexual liaisons are entered into ever more rapidly and impulsively, we need strict pastoral guidelines in order to protect one another.

When we pray 'forgive us', we acknowledge the twin realities of our sins and our sinful nature. We have an equality in our bias to selfishness. We have an equality in needing the Father's undeserved mercy. And we have an equality in needing to protect ourselves and to help one another to resist the self-destructive tendencies that, like a parasitic condition that can be controlled but not eradicated, continue to lurk within.

Personal reflection

Have you ever noticed any Pharisaical tendencies in your life? If so, how can you eradicate their pernicious influence?

2

The price of forgiveness

The Old Testament can be read as an extended education in the cost of forgiveness and the symbolic significance of blood. After the flood, Noah is given permission to enjoy an unrestricted diet, save for one consideration: 'You must not eat meat that has its lifeblood still in it' (Gen. 9:4). In preparation for the Exodus, the Jews kill the Passover lamb and spread some of its blood on the doorposts of their homes (Exod. 12). As a result, when death sweeps through Egypt in a terrible plague of infant mortality, the Jews are exempt. The lambs have become their protection, their blood the sign of redemption from the curse of divine judgment.

As the Jewish sacrificial system was developed, detailed instructions were given for the various offerings (see for example Lev. 1—4). Hands were laid on the head of the animal before it was killed, symbolising that it had come to represent the sins of the family. After the sacrifice, the blood was sprinkled against the altar: while some sacrifices could later be enjoyed as a meal, the blood was set apart as sacred. The Jews were instructed to show reverence for an animal slaughtered for the pot, draining the blood first and then covering the spillage with earth. If anyone indulged in eating blood, they were to be cut off from the nation. Blood was seen as the life-force of every creature, not to be treated casually and given a unique religious significance:

> *For the life of a creature is in the blood, and I have given it to you to make atonement for yourselves on the altar; it is the blood that makes atonement for one's life.*
>
> Leviticus 17:11

The deeply ingrained Jewish reverence for the life-blood explains the only restriction the Jewish Christians placed upon the first Gentile converts. While they were freed from any obligation to be circumcised or to embrace any other ritual requirements of the Old Testament law, apart from sexual immorality the only other restraints proposed by the Jerusalem Council were dietary:

> *You are to abstain from food sacrificed to idols, from blood, from the meat of strangled animals.*
>
> Acts 15:29

For the Jews, the impact of this emphasis upon substitutionary sacrifices and the religious significance of blood was much wider than the kitchen. Just as guilt had been transferred symbolically to an animal sacrifice by the laying on of hands,when Isaiah prophesied the decisive death of the suffering Servant, he portrayed the iniquities of the human race being laid upon God's Servant. In order to deal with the transgressions of others, the Servant would become the definitive guilt offering (Isa. 53).

John the Baptist picks up this highly familiar Jewish theme in his greeting of Jesus by the Sea of Galilee: 'Look, the Lamb of God, who takes away the sin of the world' (John 1:29). The old symbols of the sacrificial system had lost none of their power. They were coming to sharper focus in the conviction that, in one decisive sacrifice, the sins not just of a family or a nation, but the sins of all mankind could be dealt with, once for all.

The letter to the Hebrews uses a favourite Greek expression eleven times, which is translated in English as 'once' or, in an emphatic usage, 'once for all'. According to this letter, the entire Jewish sacrificial system can be seen as a massive edifice of spiritual education. The Jews had been trained for centuries in the reality of human sinfulness, the necessity of a sacrifice of atonement to be released from sin's consequences, and the significance of blood in the sacrifice.

However, the repetition of their procedures indicated an inadequacy in the entire sacrificial system. What was needed was a different order of atoning sacrifice, one that truly and definitively secured the new beginning to which the Jewish religion pointed, but which remained beyond accomplishment by means of sacrificing doves and lambs, goats and bulls. Now at last, the writer argues (some believe this letter may have been written by Priscilla, who was renowned as a great teacher of the Scriptures among the early believers), the decisive breakthrough has been secured. The entire letter is built around a pivotal contrast between the Jewish sacrificial system and the cross of Christ. For the Jews, sacrifices had to be renewed, because no sacrifice and no high priest was ever so pure as to be able to accomplish an all-sufficient rite of atonement. At the cross, however, Christ is both the impeccable high priest and the Lamb of God in perfect purity. The former sacrificial system was about endless repetition. The new atoning sacrifice is *once for all.* The old system was a mere symbol of the decisive work of God in Christ: the Jewish temple rites have therefore been rendered obsolete, surplus to requirements, now that the Lamb of God has paid the eternal price of sin.

Writing to the Romans, Paul elaborates a related, invaluable insight. Before the cross of Christ, he argues, there was a double problem with justice between humankind and God. First, the human race was in an appalling deficit before God, unable to compensate for the terrible excesses of human sin. At the same time, God was in deficit with himself. In his mercy, he had postponed exacting due retribution for the vast catalogue of human offences. But in his justice, God could not turn a blind eye for ever, pretending that sin had not happened or that it did not really matter. Christ's sacrifice of atonement is therefore doubly significant. It is God's saving initiative of mercy, as he becomes our substitute. Beyond the symbolism of the traditional animal sacrifices, he dies in our place. At the same time, it is God's saving initiative of justice, since he deals with our sin and its consequences by taking it upon himself. To use the technical language, the cross is expiatory – Christ absorbs the power of sin – and it is propitiatory – Christ absorbs the consequent judgment. At the cross, therefore, God both demonstrates his justice and becomes the justifier of the sinful. The close parallels with the ancient Jewish sacrificial system are unmistakable in Paul's deliberate choice of words:

> *God presented him as a sacrifice of atonement, through faith in his blood.*
>
> Romans 3:25

The New Testament uses many metaphors to express the impact of the cross. For example, it brings redemption to those who were enslaved; transfer from the kingdom of darkness to the kingdom of light; decisive defeat to the principalities and powers; reconciliation between God and all who put their trust in Christ, even though previously we have lived as indifferent to God or even as his enemies; justification for those who receive both forgiveness and the right standing of Christ before his Father. There is a measure of unsearchable mystery in the power of the cross, and a wonderful richness and subtlety in the variety of these metaphors. But the New Testament writers all agree about the pivotal significance of the first Easter: something happens at the cross and is completed in the resurrection of Christ, that has the power to change the eternal destiny of the human race. Forgiveness is won because the price has been paid, and it has been accomplished fully, freely and finally.

Inevitably, some Christians rather overdo their talk about blood. With a Gothic lavishness of imagination they speak at length about being washed, soaked or drenched in the blood. For those of a nervous disposition it may all seem rather garish and unpleasant. Others find the literal use of such imagery to be distasteful, even revolting, evoking scenes in an abattoir rather than the prospect of divine forgiveness. Such over-elaboration of the theme is not new. William Cowper developed the image of a fountain filled with blood and sinners plunging beneath it to be freed from every guilty stain. We may justify the poet's freedom to explore a metaphor while regretting the over-indulgence of such daring language by those without his verbal dexterity. The point in the New Testament is not that we should somehow be immersed in Christ's blood, nor is his blood said to be still flowing. Rather, he has shed his blood once for all. The innocent has died for the ungodly. The Son of God has embraced mortality so that we might enter into everlasting life. The Cross of Christ is the decisive lightning conductor for human sin and divine judgment. Its power works two ways in time, reaching backwards to the generations before the decisive saving event, and forwards even to the end of time. No further sacrifices are required, no further price need be paid. At the cross, Christ has done it all! Forgiveness has been secured irrevocably, and by faith in his atoning death, we are freed from sin's consequences for all eternity. We will still let God down, to be sure, but by faith in Christ our forgiveness remains entirely secure.

Prayer response

Pause to give thanks for the all-sufficient sacrifice of Christ.

3

Sinned against

Jesus' prayer acknowledges a double reality, and both aspects can make us feel uncomfortable. We not only continue to need God's forgiveness, we also continue to need to forgive others. King Lear's pathetic protest of impotent indignation has become the topic of countless school essays, when he cried out that he was 'a man more sinned against than sinning'. Just as it is ultimately impossible to compare precisely the two categories of sin in Lear's life, we cannot in our own. The wounded self-righteous person will always find it much easier to catalogue the sins of others than their own. Others are always apologising, even when the problem is unmistakably someone else's fault. Those with an over-tender conscience would not even consider attempting to weigh the trivial extent of the sins of others against them compared with the enormity of their own failings and offences.

In times of stress, many people find an outlet for their aggravation by having a row with their partner or closest friend. Those we love most, we are often inclined to use as involuntary lightning conductors. While some have experienced exceptionally appalling sins within their family, many more will know unresolved disputes, niggling arguments and trivial disagreements on which have been built mountains of resentment. Victims of abuse are likely to need sensitive support and counselling to come through to a place of wholeness and forgiveness. The rest of us, however, are without excuse: petty rivalries and deep-rooted resentments need to be stripped from our lives. Without a willingness to forgive others quickly, we diminish ourselves. An embittered person has become their own worst enemy, robbing themselves of wholeness today for the sake of nursing an old grievance.

Churches cannot be immune to such difficulties and every church, sooner or later, is bound to experience a measure of disagreement, difficulty and disappointment. The real issue is not that we experience disagreements at all, but how we handle such differences. Sadly, some behave in thoroughly un-Christian ways, which can cause others to feel wounded, to be tempted to retaliation, or even to become cynical. Even when attitudes remain gracious, some believers are so shocked by the very fact of a difference of opinion among Christians that they withdraw into isolation. There is no love without hurt, no closeness without vulnerability and pain.

If you are not aware of people you have needed to forgive in the past few months, you are either a very gentle spirit or you have been living in solitary confinement! Jesus is very realistic about life. Rather than suggesting that his followers could ever live in an undisturbed 'zone of harmony and contentment' where no one would ever get upset, he tells us what to do with our enmity and hostility. He minces no words. Such attitudes should be rubbed out, exterminated, obliterated beyond recall. We cannot truly pray for God's forgiveness without a determination to forgive.

In his great celebration of love, Paul identified a critical component of love that is all too easily overlooked: 'Love keeps no record of wrongs' (1 Cor. 13:5). For some people, no disagreement is complete without adding it to their mental checklist of grievances. This ensures that no argument can be brought to an end without an updated calculation: 'That's the twenty-sixth time this year that you've . . .'

Similarly, Paul advised the Colossians to 'bear with one another and forgive whatever grievances you have against one another'

(Col. 3:13). I have sometimes visited divided groups of Christians where I am quite sure that they need to become two separate churches. The differences in priorities, values or even personalities are such that their mutual incompatibility is irreversible. But the temptation is to allow this to degenerate into enmity, eagerly explaining the faults of the 'other lot' and how they are completely in the wrong. If we want to know the favour of God, we need to recognise the family likeness of all Christian believers as God's adopted children by faith in Christ. If some choose to go to a different church, or establish a new one, we should always seek to bless them in their service of Christ.

One of the greatest absurdities of the Church is to see Christians pray the Lord's Prayer together and then assail one another after the service. The weapons are usually indirect but deadly: the stiletto of gossip and the bunkers of party spirit are the favoured strategies of the divisive. But this is sheer folly. We acknowledge an equality in the mire of sin, declaring unambiguously in Jesus' words that we are sinners and that we experience wounding as a result of the sins of others. I remember preaching on reconciliation in one divided church: people from all sides thanked me for the message and went on to explain how much the other lot needed to hear it! As they pointed the finger of accusation and wielded the tongue of barbed complaint, the festering depths of divisive and destructive attitudes were unmasked. The greater offence is not to disagree in the first place, but to do so disagreeably. Even in dispute over matters of deep principle, we must seek to keep ourselves in check so that everything might be done and said in love.

The way of Jesus requires us to seek to make the first move in generosity and kindness. There are times when it may only make things worse to speak to someone about their problem with us or ours with them. When words become inadequate or inappropriate, we need the imagination to find some other way to demonstrate in action the forgiving love to which Jesus, without exception, calls his every follower.

Personal reflection

Is there anyone in particular whom you need to forgive today?

4

Motivation to forgive

Forgiveness begins not with feelings but with an act of the will. We make a determined choice to forgive. It requires a renunciation of any claim of indebtedness against those who have aggrieved us. Feelings of anger or bitterness will abate and a new, more positive, and even gentler attitude of heart will arise. But we cannot delay offering forgiveness until we have acquired the right kind of feelings. Some years ago I visited a church and saw during the communion a man walking up to receive the bread and wine who had mistreated a friend of mine several years before. He had been a games teacher and had punched one of his pupils on the back of the head to enforce discipline. It seemed to me a cowardly act twice over. First, he had sneaked up behind the pupil, landing the blow without warning. Second, it was an abuse of privilege, since there was no right under the school rules to physical self-defence against a violent teacher. These days the pupil or his parents would probably sue the school. But at that time, the power of a physically abusive teacher was almost absolute.

I had not seen the man for many years, and it had been a minor incident to which I had not given another thought. But when I saw him walking up to take communion I was incensed. For all I knew he may have repented long since of such behaviour. There was simply no way of telling. In that moment I realised that my instinctive reaction of revulsion revealed an unresolved grievance. My feelings were once again aroused against this bully. The barbs of moral indignation had lodged deep in my spirit. But now we were taking communion in the same church. Should I simply hide my feelings and ignore him in future? Jesus' uncompromising teaching could not be evaded so readily. As an act of will, I chose to forgive, relinquishing for ever my hidden attitude of heart. There was no reason to deny that his behaviour had been wrong, But my hostile attitude was equally indefensible and I needed to repent. Without repentance, it would not have been appropriate for me to receive communion that Sunday.

What, then, is our motivation to forgive? First, it is simple obedience. Jesus placed such an emphasis upon the priority of forgiveness that Peter demonstrated his own superficial grasp of his Master's priorities when he proposed as a generous new approach the responsibility to forgive someone no less than seven times. The number that in Jewish culture symbolised perfection and completeness was woefully inadequate faced with Jesus' extremism in mercy. Seventy times seven, he explained, would be rather nearer the mark. The disciples of Jesus must choose to walk in forgiveness because Jesus sets such high store by this attitude of mind and heart.

Our second motivation is the example of Jesus. In the most extreme circumstances he continued to show an absolute resolve to offer forgiveness, superlatively at the cross where he prayed for the crowd who had bayed for his blood, pleading that their ignorance of the real meaning of their actions was sufficient reason for divine mercy. How different the intemperate judgmentalism of some of the self-styled followers of Jesus! Sometimes their bile is directed against an individual who has treated them badly. At other times, a swathe of denunciation is cut through an entire denomination, because of their presumed doctrinal deficiencies, evangelistic ineffectiveness or ecclesiastical shortcomings. How perverse that the followers of the Servant King of love and forgiveness should sometimes be characterised by arrogance and hatred! Jesus prayed forgiveness for his murderers, while we can barely tolerate our fellow disciples.

Our third motivation is our own sinfulness. Jesus instructs us to grant forgiveness towards others even as we pray for mercy for ourselves. There is no escaping our own inclusion in the reality of human sin. Our motives are mixed: we commit the bad and omit the good. As a sinner in need of God's mercy, I should freely offer mercy to my fellow offenders. Those who have begun to grasp their own character flaws have no excuse for lapsing into self-righteous smugness. Those who recognise their own fallibility have no right to demand perfection from others. As those constantly dependent upon the free grace of God, we are called to be grace givers to everyone we meet. Pharisees litter life with the victims of their judgmentalism. Disciples who are sinful but true seek to rebuild damaged lives, freely expressing the forgiveness, patience and mercy that we continue to need for ourselves from our Father in heaven.

Personal reflection

Have you ever been inclined to look down on those you choose to forgive? If so, how can you avoid doing so in future?

5

The inescapable need to forgive

As soon as Jesus had provided his disciples with this new way of praying, he added a further, emphatic warning about the importance of forgiveness. There is a direct connection, he explained, between choosing to forgive others and walking in the forgiveness of our Father in heaven. If we do not forgive others, we will not be able to enjoy a right relationship with God.

The impact of unforgiveness can be even more devastating than the original offence. Frank made a vow never to forgive a bully who had made his schooldays a misery. Forty years later he was still embittered, and with the passing of years resentment had multiplied like a cancer. He was forever finding another grievance to nurse, another person who made him feel hard done by. When he finally forgave the original offender, a lifetime's enmities unravelled and the bitterness was drawn out of his heart. And when he became right with others, there was no longer a mound of nursed grievances coming between Frank and the forgiveness and love of God.

Peter had the misfortune to encounter the trivial ugliness of church politics. It had never occurred to him that church appointments mattered so much – if he had been interested in power and prestige, church was hardly the place to look for it. But when his minister preferred Peter for the role of church-warden over the previous incumbent, it was as if a dark cloud took up residence over the church.

Nothing was said directly, but when Peter came into the church lounge for coffee, one circle of friends dropped their voices and turned their backs. Others failed to return his greeting, or did so with evident reluctance. They felt that their old friend had been badly treated and that somehow it was Peter's fault. In time-honoured manner, but entirely contrary to the manner of Jesus, they cultivated their disapproval with discreet displays in public and poisonous gossip behind closed doors. Until their foolish campaign was abandoned, the whole church suffered a diminished sense of the presence of God.

For as long as Jenny refused to let go, the wounds of the past refused to heal over. Her assailant had been despicable and deserved a long stretch behind bars. But Jenny came to realise that by refusing to forgive she had become her own victim, eaten up inside by a burning anger. Worse still, because her unforgiveness built a bridge to the past, the emotional pain had never been given the opportunity to abate. It still hurt as much as when the attack first happened. No one could rewrite the past, but Jenny need not suffer as a lifelong victim. Through sensitive counselling she chose to face up not only to her anguish, but also to the self-destructive comfort of her burning anger. When she finally broke through and chose to forgive her attacker, the chains of the past dropped from her life. She was free at last, to move on and to shape a future that would no longer be imprisoned by the hurts of yesterday.

It is not a matter of earning God's forgiveness through taking the right actions. We depend upon unmerited divine mercy, demonstrated in the atoning sacrifice of Christ. His death was not for those who could save themselves, but rather for those in desperate need of a Saviour. We do not forgive others in order to win the forgiveness of God. The connections are more subtle.

First, there is the interconnectedness of life. When John emphasised the centrality of love in the Christian life, he warned that the real measure of our love for God is the amount of love we can muster for the brother or sister we love least.

If anyone says, 'I love God,' yet hates his brother, he is a liar. For anyone who does not love his brother, whom he has seen, cannot love God, whom he has not seen.

1 John 4:20

Just as the love commands that Jesus endorsed as the perfect summary of the law bring together love of God and love of one another, the two dimensions of human relationships are interconnected when it comes to forgiveness. The 'vertical' relationship to God and the 'horizontal' relationships to one another can never be treated as separate compartments, as if our relationship with God can be cultivated irrespective of the poor condition of our relationships with family, friends and colleagues. A negative attitude in one relationship spills over, contaminating or diminishing our overall capacity for love and forgiveness in every other relationship.

Second, our true intentions are revealed by our attitudes of heart. Our prayer for forgiveness is shallow for as long as we cultivate negativity towards others. We may not feel that we are going through the motions in prayer. We may object to the suggestion that our prayer for forgiveness is not in earnest. But if forgiveness really mattered to us, there would be a consonance between our attitude towards God and our attitude towards others. The person who specialises in holding grudges, nursing grievances, cataloguing the offences of others or not speaking to those who have done them wrong, has set a very low ceiling on their knowledge of God. First we must offload the deadweight of our judgmentalism. Only then can we begin to discover the depths of the forgiveness and love of God.

Third, when we become obsessed with the wrongs of others, we lose a true perspective on how much we, like they, need the forgiveness of God. We become like the foolish slave in Jesus' parable, incapable of forgiving little even when we have been forgiven much (Matt. 18:23–35). The numbers in this parable are deliberately extreme: the servant is forgiven a debt of several million pounds –

the size of a huge lottery win – but he has a man imprisoned who owes him a few pounds – a handful of small change. Resentment is typically disproportionate. Once a sense of grievance takes root, its growth is rampant, overwhelming the more tender shoots of gentleness, kindness and mercy.

Fourth, there is no hiding our negativity from God, to whom it is deeply offensive. Jesus ends the parable of the unforgiving servant with a warning about the only kind of forgiveness that is acceptable to God. Paying lip service to forgiveness is entirely unacceptable, for Jesus insists that our Father in heaven demands nothing less than that we 'forgive from the heart'. Paul makes a similar point to the Ephesians when he explains that our critical, negative, judgmental and back-biting attitudes have an immediate impact upon the Holy Spirit. They grieve the Spirit and so he withdraws from our lives.

We therefore discover two complementary truths about forgiveness in the New Testament. When considering our motivation to forgive others, Paul urges us to draw upon the example of Christ and upon the resources of the forgiveness that he has won for us:

> *Be kind and compassionate to one another, forgiving each other, just as in Christ God forgave you.*
>
> Ephesians 4:32

But Jesus emphasises the two-way traffic of forgiveness. Just as there is no better inspiration to forgive than the free gift of God's forgiveness, Jesus warns that we ration our experience of divine forgiveness by the measure with which we choose to forgive others. Jesus' words are more than a stark warning: they are also an acute diagnosis of spiritual malaise. Whenever we feel distant from God, the Lord's Prayer prompts us to self-examination: am I holding any kind of grievance against another person?

In my own spiritual experience this has proved to be a cast-iron law. When I am reluctant to forgive others, my awareness of God's love and favour are immediately diminished. If we wish to enjoy God's presence by his Spirit we must be vigilant and self-disciplined. We need to be deeply intolerant of any tendency to negativity, evicting unforgiveness without delay, whenever it attempts to take up residence in our hearts.

Personal reflection

Have you ever experienced wrong attitudes to others getting in the way of your relationship with God?

6

Declaring amnesty

Hundreds of thousands gathered in London for the funeral of Princess Diana, with millions more watching on TV. When the Lord's Prayer was announced, many began to repeat a prayer half-remembered from childhood. A nation that was grieving its lost princess was also a nation in search of lost faith. Diana had become a cultural icon. Her radiant beauty and gentle, shy touch seemed to countermand the weight of suffering in many lives, at least for a moment. Faced with her sudden and wasteful death, the flowers and candles, poems and prayers were questing after some kind of spiritual solace, some hope in the face of tragedy, some comfort in the face of despair. As everyone prayed together, for a moment at least the nation was united in the words of Jesus.

Emotional reactions pass, however intense they have been. But living faith lasts. There was a sure and immediate test of the depth with which the crowd had prayed the Lord's Prayer. If they had prayed about forgiveness and meant it, families would have been brought back from the brink, parents reconciled with children, marriages saved, friendships healed, office feuds silenced and plots for revenge abandoned in an instant.

Jesus had no interest in his followers going through the motions of forgiveness. He calls us only to discipleship, never to religious nominalism. We are not meant to pay lip service to forgiveness and then continue to berate others as if nothing had changed, nor is it enough to approve of the sentiment of forgiveness. Nor to agree with forgiveness in principle, while deferring any practical action. When the Lord's Prayer is taken seriously, the prayer becomes a lifestyle. To pray it genuinely means that we must do it. We cannot just mouth our endorsement of forgiveness, we must truly, completely and immediately forgive.

From time to time in Britain the police and politicians instigate an amnesty for knives and guns, usually after some terrible and wanton slaying of the innocents. Those who hand in their deadly – and often illegally held – weapons before a specified date are guaranteed freedom from prosecution. Because the weapons are taken off the streets for ever, the state has calculated that a universal pardon is worthwhile because of the lives that would otherwise have been put at risk. In a similar way, Jesus invites us to take part in an amnesty of negativity. He certainly does not call us to unreality, pretending that we are far too mild-mannered ever to have needed to forgive anyone at all. Even as we pray it, we should just do it. At the moment of praying about forgiveness, we are invited to relinquish all ill-feeling towards others. There are no excuses, no exceptions. It does not matter how badly we may feel we have been treated. To pray the Lord's Prayer anew is to abandon once again any grievance we have begun to nurse or any further pursuit of the revenge for which we have been longing.

I recently took an old table to the municipal refuse and recycling centre – or the dump as these places are more commonly known. It was a handsome specimen, but damaged beyond repair and worthless. It had served us well for many years, however, and just after leaving the dump I had second thoughts. Perhaps there was some way of repairing it after all, so that it could be of some use to others, even if we no longer had anywhere to put it. At once I realised this line of thought was pointless. While the table was still in our car, it belonged to the Warners. Once it was laid to rest at the dump, it was council property. Even if my second thoughts had made any sense – which they did not – I no longer had any claim to the table at all. In the same way, to pray the Lord's Prayer is to take unforgiveness to the celestial dumping ground. We offload our claims against others before the Father and that is an end of it. There is no claiming them back. When we relinquish our negativity and receive once again the embrace of the Father's love, there are no second thoughts. The old is gone. The unforgiveness is consumed. There is no right or opportunity to claim back attitudes we have asked the Father to extinguish for ever.

There are times when I am the visiting preacher at a church and an unmistakable tension crackles in the air. It may be between a couple, or between parents and children, or the entire church may be dividing into opposing parties, locked in trench warfare as futile as the battles of the First World War. If only the Lord's Prayer were taken seriously, such attitudes would be completely unsustainable. If we declare this prayer once and really mean it, the slate is wiped clean. There are no acceptable excuses. If we mean the prayer, we are simply not entitled to drag up the past and dump it on the table in a renewed dispute. We must give it to God and not try to claim it back.

In some cases it is appropriate to tell someone we have forgiven them. In others sensitivity requires that we say nothing immediately, but allow our new attitude of heart to be demonstrated in our future actions. Sadly I know people who have been emotionally abused by someone telling them they have been forgiven. Charles welcomed this promising news from Rita, who then used the positive statement like a salesman's foot in the door, proceeding to list a vast catalogue of all the misdeeds for which she had forgiven him. By the time she had finished, Charles was reeling under the immensity of his own apparent faults. But he also reluctantly concluded that the exhaustiveness of Rita's list and the enthusiastic venom with which she related every last detail were compelling evidence that she knew little of the discipline of real forgiveness.

Where there has been a history of ill-feeling in a church, the Lord's

Prayer can become the basis of an amnesty of the heart. Sometimes a long-standing disagreement within a church has become like a running sore. Sometimes a church develops a tradition of criticism and party spirit – the bone of contention may have changed several times, but the underlying attitudes are still as carping and divisive as ever. Or maybe a church has had a difficult relationship with another church in town, and has been tempted to indulge in caricature and sweeping judgments. For an Amnesty Sunday, people would be invited to write down the particular unforgiving attitude they want to leave behind. Refuse bins are provided, and the people are asked to walk up to a bin and throw away their piece of paper. Like guns handed over to the police, we hand over our destructive attitudes to God. We relinquish all claim upon them, and look for a fresh start in the forgiveness and love of God. I have seen couples put one another's names into the bin and walk away arm in arm to rebuild their marriage. Ministers' wives have forgiven churches for the tyranny of imposing a set of impossible expectations. Mothers and fathers have put in the name of a son or daughter, with whom their relationship has degenerated into the slinging of verbal shells or sullen silence. An amnesty of the heart requires careful preparation, and is unlikely to be completed without soul-searching, an inner struggle and, for many of us, not a few tears. But what a breakthrough, when we leave behind the drudgery of judgmentalism and grievance, and enter without hindrance into Jesus' lifestyle of forgiveness.

The year 2000 has been dubbed the time for 'a fresh start'. Many churches across the denominations will adopt this slogan. There is a fresh start for the developing world, tyrannised by an impossible debt burden to Western banks – an economic slavery as obscene as any trade in human flesh. There is a fresh start with God, both for those coming to faith for the first time and for believers who have got into something of a rut and need to get their spiritual act together. And there is a fresh start with one another, abandoning resentments and rivalries and renewing forgiveness and love. Jesus' teaching on forgiveness has a profound part to play in this 'fresh start'. His approach is glorious, radical and demanding. His invitation is that we should choose not merely to give verbal assent, but to seek always to live out the Lord's Prayer in practice, keeping short accounts with the Father to ensure that unforgiveness never gets a grip on our lives. The way of forgiveness is never easy, but though we may find it costly, it will also prove liberating. Jesus' perspective is unequivocal: men and women can never be truly happy until we have embraced the essential discipline of forgiveness in the manner of our Saviour.

Personal reflection

Is there anyone with whom you need an amnesty for hard feelings, a fresh start and an end to all hostility?

7

Bible Meditation

JOHN 7:53–8:11

This familiar story has much to teach about the art of forgiveness.

The teachers of the law and the Pharisees were more concerned with the principle than the person. They wanted to make a public example of the woman who had been caught in adultery. It is intriguing to speculate about what had happened to the guilty man: perhaps the Pharisees were more interested in punishing a woman or perhaps the man had shown his true attitude to the relationship by running off to save his own skin rather than making any attempt to rescue the woman. Many people have described themselves as highly principled in order to justify their refusal to forgive someone. But Jesus was never fooled by cold-heartedness.

Jesus exposed the secrets of their hearts. We are not told what Jesus wrote upon the ground. Some have speculated that he was writing quotations from the Old Testament or the names of particular sins. What is certain is that, with characteristic incisiveness, he chose just the right words to establish the universality of human sinfulness: 'Let the one without sin cast the first stone.'

One by one, the Pharisees accepted the implications of Jesus' words. The older men drifted away first, presumably unable to avoid the penetrating judgment of Jesus' words, the undeniable reality of their own moral deficiencies, and their failure once again to trap Jesus which had been the original intention of the encounter. The younger ones were more reluctant to depart, exhibiting that zeal without wisdom which has always been a hazard among young hot-heads. The history of the Christian Church is littered with the errors of those who have been quick to anger and eager to judge. Just as much as the Pharisees, Christians need to learn a wise and generous reluctance to cast the first stone.

Jesus' response to the woman gave equal expression to mercy and justice. He refused to condemn her, instead offering forgiveness and a fresh chance to make a better life. However, at the same time he described her adultery as a 'life of sin' and urged her to renounce it. The call to repentance that typifies Jesus' ministry is emphatic and unambiguous, and so is his unhesitating offer of forgiveness. Jesus reveals the God of the second chance, more interested in rescuing people than condemning them. The woman was going to be a much better example to others as a transformed individual than as a broken corpse.

Christians have been tempted to split apart the two strands of Jesus' response. Some water down Jesus' high moral standards, emphasising forgiveness but playing down the very notion of sin. Others neglect Jesus' extravagant provision of forgiveness, emphasising the need for repentance, but paying little attention to Jesus' refusal to condemn. If we are serious about the imitation of Christ, we need to explore how best to give expression, as individuals and as local churches, to his integrated combination of a call to moral purity with freely available forgiveness.

DEVOTIONAL POEMS

Sometimes a light surprises
The Christian while he sings;
It is the Lord who rises
With healing in his wings:
When comforts are declining,
He grants the soul again
A season of clear shining,
To cheer it after rain.

In holy contemplation,
We sweetly then pursue
The theme of God's salvation,
And find it ever new;
Set free from present sorrow,
We cheerfully can say,
E'en let the unknown tomorrow
Bring with it what it may.

It can bring with it nothing,
But he will bear us through;
Who gives the lilies clothing,
Will clothe his people too;
Beneath the spreading heavens
No creature but is fed;

And he who feeds the ravens
Will give his children bread.

Though vine nor fig tree neither
Their wonted fruit shall bear,
Though all the field should wither,
Nor flocks nor herds be there:
Yet God the same abiding,
His praise shall tune my voice;
For, while in him confiding,
I cannot but rejoice.

William Cowper, 1731–1800

Hark, my soul! It is the Lord;
'Tis thy Saviour, hear his word;
Jesus speaks, and speaks to thee:
'Say, poor sinner, lov'st thou me?

I delivered thee when bound,
And, when wounded, healed thy wound;
Sought thee wandering, set thee right,
Turned thy darkness into light.

Can a woman's tender care
Cease towards the child she bare?
Yes, she may forgetful be,
Yet will I remember thee.

Mine is an unchanging love,
Higher than the heights above;
Deeper than the depths beneath,
Free and faithful, strong as death.

Thou shalt see my glory soon,
When the work of grace is done;

Partner of my throne shalt be;
Say, poor sinner, lov'st thou me?'

Lord, it is my chief complaint
That my love is weak and faint;
Yet I love thee and adore,
Oh for grace to love thee more!

William Cowper

Dear Lord! Accept a sinful heart,
Which of itself complains,
And mourns, with much and frequent smart,
The evil it contains.

There fiery seeds of anger lurk,
Which often hurt my frame;
And wait but for the tempter's work,
To fan them to a flame.

Legality holds out a bribe
To purchase life from thee;
And discontent would fain prescribe
How thou shalt deal with me.

While unbelief withstands thy grace,
And puts the mercy by;
Presumption, with a brow of brass,
Says, 'Give me, or I die.'

How eager are my thoughts to roam
In quest of what they love!
But ah! When duty calls them home,
How heavily they move!

Oh! Cleanse me in a Saviour's blood,
Transform me by thy power,
And make me thy beloved abode,
And let me rove no more.

William Cowper

Oh to vex me, contraries meet in one:
Inconstancy unnaturally hath begot
A constant habit; that when I would not
I change in vows, and in devotion.
As humorous* is my contrition
As my profane love, and as soon forgot:
As ridlingly distempered, cold and hot,
As praying, as mute; as infinite, as none.
I durst not view heaven yesterday; and to day
In prayers, and flattering speeches I court God:
Tomorrow I quake with true fear of his rod.
So my devout fits come and go away
Like a fantastic Ague: save that here
Those are my best days, when I shake with fear.

John Donne

A HYMN TO GOD THE FATHER

Probably written in 1623, when a severe illness caused Donne to think that he was on the brink of death.

Wilt thou forgive that sin where I begun,
Which was my sin, though it were done before?
Wilt thou forgive that sin, through which I run,

*changeable

And do run still: though still I do deplore?
When thou hast done, thou hast not done,
For I have more.

Wilt thou forgive that sin which I have won
Others to sin? And made my sin their door?
Wilt thou forgive that sin which I did shun
A year, or two: but wallowed in, a score?
When thou hast done, thou hast not done,
For I have more.

I have a sin of fear, that when I have spun
My last thread, I shall perish on the shore;
But swear by thy self, that at my death thy son
Shall shine as he shines now, and heretofore;
And, having done that, thou hast done,
I fear no more.

CHAPTER 5

SAVE US FROM THE TIME OF TRIAL AND DELIVER US FROM EVIL

And lead us not into temptation;
but deliver us from evil

THE PULLEY

When God at first made man,
Having a glass of blessings standing by;
Let us (said he) pour on him all we can:
Let the world's riches, which dispersed lie,
Contract into a span.

So strength first made a way;
Then beauty flowed, then wisdom, honour, pleasure:
When almost all was out, God made a stay,
Perceiving that alone of all his treasure
Rest in the bottom lay.

For if I should (said he)
Bestow this jewel also on my creature,
He would adore my gifts instead of me,
And rest in Nature, not the God of Nature:
So both should losers be.

Yet let him keep the rest,
But keep them with repining restlessness:
Let him be rich and weary, that at least,
If goodness lead him not, yet weariness
May toss him to my breast.

George Herbert

1

The time of trial – circumstances

Here our two translations of the Lord's Prayer go their own ways. The traditional form emphasises temptation. The standard modern form uses a phrase with much wider implications – time of trial. We do not have to choose between these, for the original wording allows both kinds of meaning.

The modern usage – 'the time of trial' – is likely to bring to mind the law courts, perhaps testing our conscience concerning any recent parking or speeding offences. It is more appropriate to think of 'the trials of life'. The Greek word for 'temptation' can also be translated as 'testing'. It speaks therefore not only of inducements to commit sin, but also more broadly about those seasons when life becomes strained and wearisome.

I remember vividly talking to Mary, the wife of a publishing colleague from Grand Rapids in Michigan. Her new baby simply refused to sleep at night. He had apparently concluded that fortissimo screaming was a much more sensible response to the hours of darkness. Night after night Mary and Bill would take it in turns to hold the baby while walking round their apartment, in the fond hope that the movement would eventually persuade him to settle. 'When I look out over the city at 3 a.m.,' she explained, 'I feel as if I am the only person still awake in the entire metropolitan area.'

For others, the trial of life can be an intractable physical disability, recurrent depression, caring for a senile parent, never finding another job after being made redundant in mid-life, or working in a career that has taken us over so that we have little time or energy left for anything else in life. Whatever our particular circumstances, the feelings are likely to be similar for anyone feeling trapped on a treadmill with no obvious means of respite or escape. We become drained, with almost nothing left to give. At such moments, our greatest ambition may shrink to nothing more than survival. Many of these seasons of hardship prove to be quite short lived. Years later we can look back in amazement, not just at their intensity, but also at how quickly they passed. But at the time it can feel as if the demands are unrelenting, with no end in sight.

The natural human instinct is to wish to avoid such difficulties, and Jesus gives us full permission to turn our desire for an untroubled life into a request before the Father. Jesus himself, praying in Gethsemane, freely acknowledged that he would rather avoid the prospect of crucifixion. His honesty paves the way for ours. We are able to be honest with God, avoiding any attempts at spurious, pious heroism.

The request for a quiet life brings with it no guarantees. We are grateful to God whenever we become conscious of being spared from one of life's tragedies, minor or major. 'There but for the grace of God go I' is a phrase on many Christians' lips as we gratefully acknowledge our protection from someone else's hardship. But no life is immune from misfortune and suffering. Sooner or later, everyone must face a season of sorrow or pain. Many have looked to religion as a means of escape, hoping that the right devotions or the right gods will somehow give them exclusion from the common human condition. Followers of Jesus, who died prematurely in a wretchedly pain-racked public execution, have no reasonable basis for such naive expectations. The Christian God offers no immunity from suffering. Rather, when we face suffering we discover more deeply the comforting strength of the One who endured great agony on our behalf. Christian faith is not about denying the harsher realities of life, nor about escaping them, but rather about facing them squarely when they arise, strengthened with the love that will not let us go. When hardships come our way, we should never conclude that God is unable or unwilling to come to our aid. We walk the path of suffering in the company of the crucified Saviour.

The New Testament provides many rewarding insights into the good that can arise even in the depths of hardship. Peter used the metaphor of purified gold (1 Pet. 1:7). Even as gold is purified by fire, our faith is refined by suffering. It is tested, not to destruction but in order to be proved genuine. The way of suffering, according to Peter, can become a means of vindicating and strengthening our faith.

Paul even dared to speak of rejoicing in sufferings (Rom. 5:2–4). This was not due to some perversely masochistic tendency, but because he traced the benefits of hardship: suffering produces perseverance; perseverance, character; character, hope. In the hands of God, Paul dares to argue, the straw of human tragedy can be woven into the gold of a noble character, capable of standing up for the good, whatever our personal circumstances. This ladder of ascent rises from its source in suffering to its summit in the love of God. We do not undergo this transformation in isolation, he confidently assures the Roman church, because God's love is poured into our hearts (Rom. 5:5). In the midst of suffering, God's presence breaks out within us. We not only look back with hope to the resurrection of Christ, beyond the day of suffering, but even in our hardest moments there is the prospect of experiencing a fresh, inward encounter with the sustaining power of divine love.

Paul explained to the Colossians that the power of God makes a distinctive contribution in the hour of suffering (Col. 1:11). Naturally we would prefer no suffering to arise, but when it does, the power of God is not annulled. He speaks of being strengthened by God's glorious might in two complementary ways: for great endurance, which means the strength to put up with difficult circumstances; and for great patience, which means the strength to put up with difficult people. In short, there is no season of life in which we are bereft of divine resources. We may struggle to cope with life in extremis, but we are never alone.

These insights from the apostolic age greatly enrich our understanding of Jesus' prayer. In easier days we pray for divine mercy, that we may be protected from hardship. But if we must face a harsher season of life, the prayer still rings true as we continue to request God's protection. An upper limit is set to our suffering that we might continue to hold up under it, strengthened by the supportive presence of heavenly love.

Personal reflection

In what aspect of life do you feel most in need of God's protection at present?

2

The time of trial – persecution

The broad plea for protection from hardship takes on a sharper edge in the context of persecution. Just as every experience of suffering is a time of testing for our faith, a period of systematic, state-sponsored persecution would test us acutely. It is difficult for Western Christians to imagine this prospect, for we have lived free from significant persecution for generations.

It is an ironic stupidity of the Western Church that most persecution of Christians has been by other Christians. At the time of the Reformation, the state church Protestants persecuted the Catholics, who persecuted the Protestants with equal vigour. And both groupings assaulted those Christians with no ties to any state authorities – the Anabaptists, who practised believers' baptism and urged a radical separation of Church and State. The favoured method was drowning, with the perverse logic that those with such a partiality for immersion would surely enjoy another dose of the same. It is a curious twist of Christian history that while the dominant churches of Western Europe are still perceived to be the Catholics and the state church Protestants, in the global Church the believer-baptising movement survived this universal persecution and now comprises the Baptists, Pentecostals and countless smaller groupings, representing several of the largest denominations in the world and some of the most vigorous contributors to the worldwide growth of the Church.

The early Church knew nothing of the perversity of Christian killing Christian. Their persecutors fiercely opposed any expression of this new religion out of Galilee. At times persecution was local. Luke records instances of Jewish synagogue leaders provoking a crowd against the apostles, but also of Gentile silversmiths rioting in protest that this new religion threatened their trade by undermining the power of paganism. Before long, in the dark days of Nero and Domitian, the Roman Empire made its first attempts at more systematic elimination of the 'followers of the way'. The early Christian writings are filled with heroic deaths, by young and old, by women and men. Their experiences even shifted the meaning of a Greek word, for the Greek word for 'witness' – and it was naturally for their witness that the first Christians faced torture and death – became the source for the English word 'martyr', meaning no longer simply a witness, but one who remains faithful to Christ, even to the point of death.

Once again, Jesus encourages us to be brutally frank before the Father. Only a fool would relish the prospect of persecution. Jesus invites his followers to pray that they may be spared such a prospect. At the same time he warns them not to be surprised by future persecution: if the Master's fate is persecution, his servants can hardly expect a better prospect (John 15:20). To be persecuted on account of Jesus is to be blessed (Matt. 5:11). Following Jesus' example, we should pray for our persecutors (Matt. 5:44). When facing a law court, Jesus promised that the Holy Spirit would supply the necessary words for us to speak.

Beyond the universal prospect of intermittent persecution lies the prospect of an intensified time of trial in the last days (Luke 21:9–36). Jesus warned that believers will be betrayed by family and friends, hated by every nation, seized, imprisoned, taken before kings and governors, persecuted and finally executed. But even this dread prospect is not without its more positive perspective. By the Spirit,

Jesus will provide the last generation with words of wisdom that no adversary will be able to resist or contradict. And the public trials of Christians will result in kings and governors hearing the good news that might otherwise never have reached their ears.

There is an unavoidable tension for Christians about the last days. On the one hand we pray with the first generation, 'Maranatha – Oh Lord, come quickly!' Yet at the same time we pray that God might preserve us from that final, cataclysmic time of trial. In our frailty, we seek divine protection. But if the days of persecution engulf the Church, believers can look to the crucified and risen Christ to bring to birth renewed faith and hope. Naturally we would far rather be preserved from martyrdom, and so we can pray with vigour to be spared from such a day, but even that terrifying prospect cannot overcome our inextinguishable hope in the God of the resurrection.

Prayer response

Pause for a moment to pray for the persecuted Church around the world.

3

A time of temptation

We turn now from trials to temptations, the second aspect of Jesus' phrase. As a teenager, this was the part of the Lord's Prayer that had me perplexed. To ask God not to lead us into temptation sounded like a small child asking a malevolent big brother not to scare them in the dark. Does this mean that God habitually takes the initiative in leading us into sin, but we can try to persuade him to leave us alone? Such a suggestion could not be further from the truth. The modern English version of the Lord's Prayer captures the essential meaning of the original expression by using the word 'save'. This is not a prayer for gentle treatment, but a request for protection. God most certainly never tempts us, but he does have the authority to set limits on the work of the tempter.

The psychological dynamics of temptation are explored brilliantly in Genesis 3. Three reasons are given for ignoring God's law. First, Eve is asked whether God ever really issued the restriction. In other words, she is invited to reinterpret God's law to mean the opposite of its apparent intent. Second, Eve is told that the fruit will not be deadly, despite God's warning. That is, the consequences that were the cause of the restriction in the first place are dismissed out of hand. Third, Eve is told that the fruit will make her like God (Gen. 3:1–5). That is, far from doing her harm, the fruit will enrich her life, and at the same time God's motives are impugned, even suggesting that the law is hypocritical, since the restriction has been issued, according to Satan, not to protect the innocent but to preserve God's own power. We can trace an almost identical sequence in the pressure to use illicit drugs: surely the law turns a blind eye to recreational drugs, now that 'everyone' is using them; the dangers of their use have been greatly exaggerated; the benefits are literally ecstatic, and anyway today's senior politicians and judges were all taking illegal drugs back in the sixties. Specious arguments in favour of sin have always been seductive.

The cumulative impact of such temptations can begin to seduce the mind, encouraging us to dismiss out of hand any restrictions upon our behaviour. The writer of Genesis then provides a second sequence, as temptation begins to take root (Gen. 3:6). This time the process of temptation moves on from rationalising away God's law to being drawn into the allure of the illicit action. Eve sees that the fruit was 'good for food' – she discovers an appetite for the snack in prospect – it is 'pleasing to the eye' – she lets her gaze begin to dwell upon it longingly – and it is 'desirable for gaining wisdom' – the prospect of wisdom is a return to rationalisation, for the operative word is 'desirable', signifying that a passionate longing is quickening in Eve's heart for the forbidden fruit. Like the willing victim of a modern advertising campaign, Eve has been seduced into longing for something for which she previously had no desire at all. This sequence can also be seen in other temptations. The teenager looks at the offered tablet and concludes that it looks harmless enough, they cannot take their eyes away from it, and they find increasingly desirable the amazing sensations that the dealer has promised. Before they hand over their money, they are already burning with an eager longing to swallow the pill as soon as possible.

The letter to the Hebrews speaks of Jesus being 'tempted in every way just as we are' (Heb. 4:15). This remarkable statement tells us that there was no pretence about Jesus' humanity. His was real humanity, subject to the normal appetites and cravings. And yet, the writer adds immediately, he was 'without sin'. The implications of this assertion are profound. First, Jesus' temptations were not restricted to the time in the wilderness after his baptism. That was undoubtedly a pivotal moment, at the beginning of his public ministry, but the experience of being tempted, presumably in a wider variety of ways, was evidently sustained throughout his life. Second, there is a fundamental distinction to be drawn between temptation and sin. Since Jesus was without sin, then to be tempted is not in itself a sin. Third, as Hebrews emphasises, Jesus is able to sympathise with us in our weakness, because he shares our humanity and our experience of being tempted, even though he demonstrated a consistent defiance of temptation which has proved to be beyond the best of his followers.

Just as we need to understand the dynamics of temptation and the vital distinction between temptation and sin, we need also to be clear that failure does not result in instant dismissal from the family of God. That does not mean that we treat sin lightly. But however seriously we take our sins, the gospel demands that we take the grace of Christ even more seriously.

This, surely, is the most important implication of Peter's betrayal at the time of Jesus' trial (Mark 14:66–72). Stunned by Jesus' arrest, Peter follows him as far as he can, at great personal risk. But when he is directly confronted by the suggestion that he is one of Jesus' followers, self-preservation swings into gear. Peter denies that he knows Jesus and covers his tracks with a liberal sprinkling of curses. When Jesus had warned him about the threefold denial, Peter had been horrified, immediately rejecting such a wretched prospect. But when the power of Jerusalem and Rome was mobilised against his Master, the flaw in his character made Peter bend before temptation like a young sapling before a hurricane. He yielded without resistance before its force. Once he had taken the easy way out, the cock crowed the final time even as Jesus had prophesied. Then Peter broke down and wept, appalled at the pathetic weakness of his lack of resolve.

Peter's devastating failure is not, of course, the end of his discipleship. The risen Christ appears to him personally and recommissions him for leadership in the Church. Peter was no doubt profoundly chastened by the discovery of his own character defects, but that may even have made him a better leader in the future. The decisive factor, however, was not his failure but the response of Christ. He is the God of the second chance. Slow to give up on us, he is willing to forgive even extreme failure like Peter's. Here then are two glorious principles: to be tempted is not to sin, and we can learn to say no; but when we do give in, restoration is but a prayer away, for the risen Christ is full of mercy towards his weak-willed and changeable disciples.

Personal reflection

The writer of Genesis explored the beguiling and seductive power of temptation in Eve's life. Have you ever been able to trace a similar pattern in your own experience?

4

The way of escape

To ask for God to preserve us from temptation is to acknowledge our own weakness. If we cannot be protected entirely from temptation, at least we can pray for God to limit the temptations that cross our path. 'Lead us not into temptation' is a prayer for patient protection. The Father has a much better idea of our limitations than we do, and so we ask him to take account of our deficiencies and limit accordingly the temptations that we face from day to day.

The apostle Paul explored this thought when writing to the Corinthians:

> *No temptation has seized you except what is common to men and women. And God is faithful; he will not let you be tempted beyond what you can bear. But when you are tempted, he will also provide a way out so that you can stand up under it.*
>
> 1 Corinthians 10:13

First, Paul emphasises the banality of temptation. Although people sometimes make excuses for themselves, as if the pressures they have come under were unique, Paul insists that temptation is a standard bill of fare: the menu from which our particular temptations are drawn is predictable and familiar. Second, Paul emphasises the faithfulness of God. He does not exclude every temptation from our experience, for that would remove the possibilities of personal growth into maturity by learning to resist temptations that once had an immediate and tyrannous grip upon our lives. What is provided is an upper limit upon temptation – we will not be assailed to the point of irreversible inner collapse.

The word Paul uses also conveys the meaning of pressure. There are seasons of life that become very pressured indeed, and at such times this promise becomes a lifeline: I may be stretched thin, but God will not allow me to be taken entirely beyond the limits of my inner resources. This promise of divine protection should not be turned upon its head. Some of the most vulnerable people, who genuinely feel that they can no longer cope with their circumstances, find it easy to blame and castigate themselves. The walking wounded often need sustained help from others so that they can learn to treat themselves with the kindness and patience with which they are viewed by their Father in heaven. Even as the risen Christ rebuilt Peter's shattered self-respect after his threefold denial, he still comes to restore broken lives today.

Paul's most important insight into the dynamics of resisting temptation is saved till the end of this glorious promise. Not only will God set an upper limit to our temptations that is appropriate to our individual resources, he will also provide a 'way out'. My parents live in a North Devon coastal village which is reached by crossing Exmoor. The moorland sits high over the narrow coastal strip, and the road becomes a steep incline, plunging down towards sea level. The warning signs insist that drivers engage a low gear and test their brakes, but an additional provision has to be made for heavy lorries. Beside the road is an escape track, thickly covered in gravel, into which a runaway lorry will quickly sink and be brought to a sudden halt. Without the escape track, the precarious road would be far too dangerous for road hauliers to supply the shops on the coastal strip. In a similar way, God makes life safer by providing a way out. Even when we are on the brink of a runaway response to temptation, we can still take the escape route rather than careening out of control. The options stay open, if only we will choose to avoid the way of least resistance.

In order to take advantage of God's escape routes, it helps to recognise the kinds of temptation to which we are particularly susceptible. Most people can detect in their lives a pattern of recurrent weaknesses – an Achilles heel where we would be wise to shore up our defences. The ancient monastic vow gives us a clear indication of three common arenas of temptation – poverty, chastity and obedience. I am not for one moment suggesting that today's Christians should all embrace a monastic lifestyle. But poverty speaks of the temptations of love of money and materialism. Chastity speaks of the temptations of casual and impulsive sexual relations outside the marriage bond. And obedience speaks of the temptations of pride, self-assertiveness (whether physical or through doing others down through gossip and back-biting) and also the determination to go our own way, irrespective of the wise counsel of others.

Sometimes the escape route is as predictable as the temptation. If a particular shop provokes temptation, do not walk past it. If a particular TV programme is a problem, do not watch it. In the workplace or among friends, do not succumb to the pressure that 'everyone's doing it'. If a married person begins to confide in you more deeply than they confide in their partner, or indeed if they begin to tell you the failings of their partner, they are already dabbling with a kind of emotional adultery, and it would be wise to avoid opportunities for such conversations in future. If such 'emotional adultery' tends to happen over a working lunch, it is time to start having lunch elsewhere!

If we are serious about praying the Lord's Prayer, we are asking God to limit the temptations that come our way. But this can never absolve us from responsibility. Having prayed for protection, we need to protect ourselves. The precarious steps from temptation to sin are swiftly and easily taken. We need to be alert to the escape routes God has promised to provide.

Personal reflection

What very practical 'way of escape' can you choose to take to avoid a common temptation?

5

The reality of evil

When we were children, my younger brother was scared by the Daleks. The greatest enemies the BBC ever created for Dr Who were designed to strike terror into countless children. Some of my friends were only able to watch while taking cover behind a chair. One of the luxuries of the imagination is to experience the frisson of such a terror, at once non-existent and yet utterly compelling. For several years our landing light was left on every night as the final line of self-defence. I never did quite grasp how the conquerors of the universe could be so confidently repelled by 100 watts . . .

Mention the devil and Western minds are filled with medieval imagery. Ghastly twisted faces, often blood red and topped with horns, are linked with pointed tails and three-pronged forks. Such macabre, gargoylian excesses are more likely to amuse than strike terror into an adult. Surely Jesus is not inviting us to pray about such outmoded superstitions?

Just as our notions of eternal judgment have been gravely distorted by medieval representations, our culture has trivialised evil. First we clothed it in fanciful costumes. Then we concluded that we were far too sophisticated to give credence to such creatures of the night.

One of the most vivid encounters with evil that I have ever known was in Berlin. Shortly after the great dividing wall had been destroyed and the old city united once again, I had the privilege to walk among the last ruined vestiges of the Communist and Fascist empires, before the developers swept in to build the new commercial centre around Potsdamerplatz. In a small museum set among the grounds where Nazi headquarters had once stood, there was a photographic display of the excesses of the Führer. In my eyes, the epitome of evil was not the small man in the big hat, but the adulation of ordinary people. In one photo a woman rushed out from the crowd, her arm thrust high in the Nazi salute. Her face was rapt with devotion. Far more intense than today's fans greeting the latest pop idol, her radiant expression, more eloquent than words, showed plainly and unreservedly that Hitler was her Messiah, the Saviour of the German nation. Beyond the manipulative cunning of the lovers of power who made up the Nazi court, far more disturbing than the unthinking obedience of young men in the military, that young mother's devotion summed up for me the power of evil. So entrancing, so compelling was the sheer force of the Nazi myth, that evil had become her good.

There is in the brute excesses of such regimes an evil that transcends the normal boundaries of human wickedness. A similar evil stalked the killing fields of Cambodia, where a show of affection or the possession of spectacles could be taken as evidence of anti-Communist tendencies. Something overtakes ordinary people in such times. Excesses from which they would otherwise shrink become their stock in trade. There is no better explanation of such appalling nightmares than a brooding evil force, which seizes such opportunities to strip entire nations of their human dignity. In smaller ways, this same force is seen in the wanton barbarism that fills headlines and provokes journalists to ask whether we are reaching the end of Western civilisation: road rage that turns a traffic violation into a murder; a gang of girls consumed with anger who kick a classmate to death; young children who take away an even younger child and kill him; the crazed gunmen who seek to kill every child in sight.

To speak of a 'personal' devil is to abuse language. He – or rather it – is fundamentally anti-personal, the very antithesis of a personal

God. Made in the image of God, human beings are the particular objects of evil's hatred and contempt. To strip us of our dignity, to eradicate our capacity for love and goodness, is to deface the image of God. This force, according to Jesus, is an undeniable reality, deeply antagonistic to the love, mercy and righteousness of the living God. But there is no place for dualism in the Bible: the force of evil is no match for the goodness of God. Like vandals smashing up a shopping mall, evil loves to disfigure men and women, but Christ's cross and resurrection have won the decisive battle. The New Testament describes Satan as a roaring lion, but this lion is chained. The Christian who fails to recognise the power of evil may take risks with his destructive talons. But the believer who overstates the power of evil does favours only to Satan. Jesus proposes a simple prayer – 'deliver us' – not an elaborate liturgy of spiritual warfare. James is equally confident that through the triumph of the cross, Christ is our great protector. Resist the devil, he explains, and he will quite simply have no option but to flee from you (Jas. 4:7).

The modern Church prefers extremism to this biblical moderation. Some sniff with disdain at the very mention of Satan. Their theology is too sophisticated, their church life far too well mannered for any such talk to be tolerated in polite, religious company. These are the cultured despisers of the perspective and piety of Jesus. At the opposite extreme are the affficionados of elaborate schemes of spiritual warfare. With complex ways of praying, exotic testimonies and sometimes even detailed diagrams of the working of evil, these enthusiasts for confronting dark forces go into far more detail than the New Testament, devoting much energy to seeking to identify and confront ruling spirits in a way without precedent in the apostolic age. It is always difficult to examine such approaches objectively without the risk of causing offence, or even seeming to be 'on the other side'. But the enthusiasts for such approaches need to take care that they avoid the kind of speculative super-spirituality that Paul roundly condemned in his letter to the Colossians. They also need to be able to explain why, if their methods guarantee the success they often claim, there is no evidence of their being used either by Christ himself, or by the advancing Church of the apostolic age. If Paul could establish a church in Ephesus, the centre of the Diana cult, without the need for the more exotic approaches of modern 'spiritual warfare', we are obliged to question whether such methods may not be surplus to the spiritual equipment of biblical Christians. At their worst, the more intense approaches seem more exotic than genuinely beneficial – a kind of super-spiritual mumbo-jumbo, full of sound and fury, signifying very little at all.

The approach of the Lord's Prayer is simple and direct. We pray for the Father to deliver us from evil. There is no attempt to specify the particular brand of evil, nor any need to address evil directly. We seek the Father's protection and then live in renewed confidence that it has been granted. There is no complication and no fuss. Jesus invites us neither to dismiss the reality of supernatural evil, nor to get hung up about it. In a brief sentence, the power of evil is bound, and we turn to concentrate upon the positive praying that matters most.

Prayer response

Give thanks to the risen Christ for the triumph of his Cross over every kind of evil.

6

Principalities and powers

As well as this general desire to be protected from evil, there are three further dimensions of demonic influence acknowledged within the Bible. First, Satan is the ultimate source of temptation. While God sets limits to evil and uses our victories over temptation to purify and reinforce our faith, we see in the temptations of Jesus a systematic attempt to demean and destroy all goodness. Previously we observed the psychology of temptation in Genesis. Jesus' temptations reveal two further principles. First, it is just after Jesus' baptism and his anointing by the Spirit for public ministry that he experiences a period of intense temptation: spiritual highs are all too often followed by spiritual lows. It may even be that we are at our most vulnerable just after something very positive has happened in our lives. Second, Satan's method with Jesus is to twist Scripture, trying to suggest that the biblical revelation can be reinterpreted as a manual of self-centredness and self-indulgence. Jesus was not easily fooled, but the witness of history suggests that his followers have been more susceptible to a reinterpretation of the Bible in ways that seem to justify our selfishness. Of course, the reality of a tempter who opposes us gives us no excuses faced with recurrent sin. Our failures are not his fault but ours. Sin requires an act of will that we make for ourselves. There can be no buck-passing: it may be the tempter who tempts, but it is always the sinner who sins.

The second dimension of demonic influence is demon possession. The Gospels are in no doubt that people can fall prey to direct demonic infiltration that can contaminate and distort their lives. We need to make a precise distinction between Galilee and Hollywood. Today's horror movies take a macabre delight in portraying 'demonic *possession*', in which human beings are completely taken over and even destroyed by evil. They become like a ventriloquist's dummy in the hands of a higher power. But the New Testament uses a much more restrained term – '*demonisation*'. This suggests a parasitic presence, not a hostile and comprehensive takeover.

Similarly, horror movies and tabloid newspapers love to talk about '*exorcism*', with the suggestion of a prolonged and tortuous confrontation between the demons and the exorcist, an uneven contest which usually favours the forces of darkness. In the New Testament the emphasis is upon a decisive battle that has already been won by the risen Christ. It is, as the old hymn celebrated, the demons who have to fear and fly when confronted with the name of Jesus. Just as demonisation is a more moderate concept than 'demon possession', the New Testament does not speak of 'exorcism', but rather of '*casting out*'. The expulsion is swift and certain whenever Jesus confronts evil.

We see Jesus' confident authority carried through into the ministry of the first apostles – not, of course, in their case based upon a spiritual self-confidence, but rather upon an undimmed confidence in the name of Jesus. Just as the first Christians baptised in the name of Jesus and prayed in the name of Jesus, their leaders cast out demons in the same victorious name. When Paul was church-planting at Philippi, his team suffered daily distraction when a slave girl known for her fortune-telling prowess kept following them, shouting, 'These men are servants of the Most High God, who are telling you the way to be saved' (Acts 16:16–18). Strikingly, she tells the truth, but in such a way as to trouble the team and distract their potential audience. Rather than dealing with the problem immediately, Paul attempts to ignore her and it is only after many days of persistent distraction that he eventually determines to deal with the demon. His words are terse: 'In the name of Jesus Christ I command you to come out of her!' – and the result is immediate. The spirit promptly departs and the girl's fortune-telling ability evaporates.

For Paul demons are a troubling distraction, not a menace that will provoke sleepless nights. They are dealt with briskly and never allowed to become centre stage in his ministry. In Ephesus, a Jewish family of professional exorcists, the sons of Sceva, were so impressed by Paul's methods that they tried to emulate his success with these words, 'In the name of Jesus, whom Paul preaches, I command you to come out.' Unimpressed by this attempt to employ a secondhand technique without personal faith, the demon mocks these men and then the man with the spirit overpowers them and gives them a beating, so that they run from the house naked and bleeding (Acts 19:13–16). By including this episode, Luke establishes several important principles: Christian deliverance ministry requires personal faith in Christ; a demonised person may be prone to dangerous, violent excess; those who dabble in such a ministry run the risk of personal humiliation and harm – although even here we should note the moderation of the New Testament, since the sons of Sceva are merely left naked and bleeding rather than suffering any of the graphic and gothic excesses of a Hollywood thriller.

One final observation about deliverance ministry is crucial: it is nowhere suggested in the New Testament that deliverance is an activity in which every Christian should be eager to get involved, like a band of trigger-happy gunslingers. Dealt with quickly and without any hint of glamour or sensation, this is a secondary ministry of Christian leadership. In today's pastoral ministry, a wise and responsible diagnosis needs to be made as to whether the presenting symptoms indicate a psychological or spiritual problem, since an inappropriate response is likely to make matters worse for the sufferer. Sensible advice for most Christians is simply this: there really is no need for you to get involved.

The third aspect of evil influence in the New Testament is significantly different from personal temptation and personal deliverance ministry. Writing to the Ephesians, Paul speaks of our struggle not with flesh and blood, but with the 'rulers', 'authorities', 'powers of this dark world' and 'the spiritual forces of evil in the heavenly realms'. A broad consensus has developed that these powers should be seen as the origin of 'structural sin'. For example, black people in Britain today face two very different kinds of racism. There is the overt, hate-spitting racism of the tiny minority of extreme nationalists. But there is also the pervasive and pernicious influence of unconscious, structural racism, which results in black people still suffering discrimination in education, employment and the law courts. Although some of this discrimination may arise from overt racists, much is an unconscious cultural legacy, in which people who would certainly not describe themselves as racists behave with unconscious prejudice towards those with a different colour skin. What is true of racism is equally true of sexism: there is a cultural legacy of prejudice that we need to learn to offload.

Similar dehumanising tendencies can also be traced in the gargantuan debt crisis of the developing world: it is not that Western governments or banks have deliberately conspired to crush the poorest countries under an unsustainable burden of interest. Fair-minded bankers find themselves part of a system that is unintentionally pernicious, condemning nations to an inescapable exclusion from wealth, health and well-being. Institutions, political systems and cultures can take on a life of their own, in which normal human decency is crushed and eliminated, and people without power become mere pawns and helpless victims.

Paul gave absolutely no encouragement to any presumptuous attempt at a head-on collision with such powers. He emphasised four means by which our spiritual struggle is advanced: by standing firm in the truth of the gospel; by standing firm in the values of the gospel, notably righteousness, peace and faith; by declaring the good news of the triumph of the cross of Christ, where the powers were stripped of their pretended authority; and by praying in the Spirit at all times (Eph. 6:13 ff.; Col. 2:15).

When we pray to be delivered from evil, the succinct request of Jesus' prayer naturally encompasses every aspect of the influence of such powers. We ask for protection from the pressures of the tempter, from invasive demonic influences, and from institutional and cultural influences that tend to dehumanise both the exploited and their exploiters. Such a prayer calls us to active struggle: for all of us to seek to resist temptation, for church leaders to ensure the provision of appropriate deliverance ministry, and for all of us to campaign against the pernicious influence of structural sin, wherever it may be exposed.

We should end this chapter on a positive note. This section of Jesus' prayer gives no justification for a nervous, anxious, let alone intense or hysterical attitude. We ask for protection with confidence, because we pray to the God of love, who is passionately concerned with our well-being, and we pray in the name of Jesus, whose death and resurrection demonstrate that he is *Christus Victor* – the one who has decisively triumphed, once for all, over evil in all its abhorrent forms.

Prayer response

Pray against the tyrannous debt-enslavement of the developing world by the Western banking system. You may also want to research the latest statistics and write a letter to leading politicians.

7

Bible Meditation

MATTHEW 26:36–46

The Gospel-writers made no effort to conceal the agonies of spirit with which Jesus faced the prospect of death. They were not embarrassed by the full humanity of Jesus, nor did they feel any need to recast Jesus' last evening of freedom as if he was entirely serene and untroubled. Jesus described himself as 'overwhelmed with sorrow to the point of death'. The Gospels present him as 'deeply distressed' (Mark 14:33), 'sorrowful', 'troubled' (Matt. 26:37) and 'in anguish' (Luke 22:44). His sweat fell to the ground like 'drops of blood' (Luke 22:44). We may presume that it was not simply the prospect of death that almost overwhelmed him, but the realisation that he would suffer nothing less than total separation from God himself as he became the atoning sacrifice for human sin.

Gethsemane is on the Mount of Olives, just across the valley from the Temple Mount. The city where Jesus was soon to be crucified was therefore in full view as he sought renewed strength from his Father. Jesus' prayer at Gethsemane passes through two vitally important stages. First, he acknowledges his distress and expresses his instinctive personal preference that he might be spared from imminent death. Second, he reaffirms his willing obedience, submitting anew to the wisdom and will of God.

Jesus is self-aware, in touch with his own feelings rather than rushing headlong towards his death in a kind of emotional self-oblivion. He gives no place to denial, preferring freely to reveal his distress to his closest friends. In his suffering, Jesus therefore gives his followers full permission to get real with God. There is no need for false heroics, no obligation to mask our true feelings. When a time of trial seems fit to overwhelm us, there need be no holds barred as we bring our emotional crisis before our Father in heaven.

Even as he demonstrates that expressing our emotions before God is healthy, Jesus also reveals that it is insufficient. Beyond his instinctive emotional desire to escape a time of trial is a decisive act of will as Jesus moves from an expression of distress and vulnerability to a renewed act of obedient submission. In imitation of Christ, we too are called to a double wisdom – not only a healthy, emotional openness in prayer, but also a willing surrender to the purposes of God. In the end, the Father knows best.

The way of the Cross is integral to Jesus' obedience. Faith in Christ therefore cannot possibly offer some kind of immunity from suffering. When a Christian faces extreme hardship, faith in the crucified Saviour will sustain them. Jesus' example at Gethsemane invites us not to evade suffering, but to walk in the way of the Cross, strengthened by God's supportive presence.

DEVOTIONAL POEMS

GOD'S GRANDEUR

The world is charged with the grandeur of God.
It will flame out, like shining from shook foil;
It gathers to a greatness, like the ooze of oil
Crushed. Why do men then now not reck his rod?
Generations have trod, have trod, have trod;
And all is seared with trade; bleared, smeared with toil;
And wears man's smudge and shares man's smell: the soil
Is bare now, nor can foot feel, being shod.

And for all this, nature is never spent;
There lives the dearest freshness deep down things;
And though the last lights of the black West went
Oh, morning, at the brown brink eastward, springs –
Because the Holy Ghost over the bent
World broods with warm breast and with ah! bright wings.

Gerard Manley Hopkins, 1844–89

SPRING

Nothing is so beautiful as Spring –
When weeds, in wheels, shoot long and lovely and lush;
Thrush's eggs look little low heavens, and thrush
Through the echoing timber does so rinse and wring
The ear, it strikes like lightnings to hear him sing;
The glassy pear tree leaves and blooms, they brush
The descending blue; that blue is all in a rush
With richness; the racing lambs too have fair their fling.

What is all this juice and all this joy?
A strain of the earth's sweet being in the beginning
In Eden garden. – Have, get, before it cloy,
Before it cloud, Christ, lord, and sour with sinning,
Innocent mind and Mayday in girl and boy,
Most, O maid's child, thy choice and worthy the winning.

Gerard Manley Hopkins

No worst, there is none. Pitched past pitch of grief,
More pangs will, schooled at forepangs, wilder wring.
Comforter, where, where is your comforting?
Mary, mother of us, where is your relief?
My cries heave, herds-long; huddled in a main, a chief
Woe, world-sorrow; on an age-old anvil wince and sing –
Then lull, then leave off. Fury had shrieked 'No ling-
ering! Let me be fell: force I must be brief.'

O the mind, mind has mountains; cliffs of fall
Frightful, sheer, no-man-fathomed. Hold them cheap
May who ne'er hung there. Nor does long our small
Durance deal with that steep or deep. Here! creep,
Wretch, under a comfort serves in a whirlwind: all
Life death does end and each day dies with sleep.

Gerard Manley Hopkins

Once I turned from thee and hid,
Bound on what thou hadst forbid;
Sow the wind I would; I sinned:
I repent of what I did.

Bad I am, but yet thy child.
Father, be thou reconciled,
Spare thou me, since I see
With thy might that thou art mild.

I have life before me still
And thy purpose to fulfil;
Yea a debt to pay thee yet:
Help me, sir, and so I will.

Gerard Manley Hopkins

Spit in my face, you Jews, and pierce my side,
Buffet, and scoff, scourge and crucify me,
For I have sinned, and sinned, and only he,
Who could do no iniquity, hath died:
But by my death can not be satisfied
My sins, which pass the Jews' impiety:
They killed once an inglorious man, but I
Crucify him daily, being now glorified;
Oh let me then, his strange love still admire:
Kings pardon, but he bore our punishment.
And Jacob came cloth'd in vile harsh attire
But to supplant, and with gainful intent:
God cloth'd himself in vile man's flesh, that so
He might be weak enough to suffer woe.

John Donne

CHAPTER 6

FEEDING ON CHRIST BY FAITH

The meaning and power of the Lord's Supper

TRINITY SUNDAY

Lord, who hast formed me out of mud,
And has redeemed me through thy blood,
And sanctified me to do good;

Purge all my sins done heretofore:
For I confess my heavy score,
And I will strive to sin no more.

Enrich my heart, mouth, hands in me,
With faith, with hope, with charity;
That I may run, rise, rest with thee.

George Herbert

1

A meal for the undeserving

As a teenager I was involved in setting up summer Bible study groups for a large youth club. At the end of the summer we set aside an evening to discuss how people felt about communion. It was not something we had talked about together before. In most churches communion is simply something that happens: we rarely have an opportunity to discuss its meaning or what it does for us, spiritually or emotionally.

The discussion rapidly centred upon a single emotional response. One after another those teenagers acknowledged that they always felt that they did not deserve to take communion. Unworthiness almost overcame them just before it was their turn to eat and drink. Those churches that have communicants wait in line to receive have an advantage with this particular response. As we stand in the queue, there is time for sober reflection. The momentary delay reinforces our desire to take communion, but it also provokes a period of self-examination.

If our understanding of communion is distorted, this mood of unworthiness may become unhelpful. Those who think that we are saved by our own best efforts may attempt to shore up their faltering efforts, putting on a brave face in order to suggest that they really are making the grade as a self-saved Christian. But the very notion of saving ourselves is quite alien to the New Testament. While Jesus called the first disciples to follow him, making determined efforts to pursue the life of discipleship, he also spoke of the necessity of his atoning death – 'as a ransom for many' (Mark 10:45). As the letter to the Ephesians resoundingly affirms, it is by grace that we are saved, through faith, and this comes not from ourselves but as God's gift. Our good deeds make no contribution, so there is no place for boasting (Eph. 2:8–9).

A very different distortion of communion is found among those who emphasise guilt, repentance and confession but lose sight of forgiveness, reconciliation and joy. They create a climate where communion is a dark and brooding experience, more to be endured than enjoyed. A church that has more to say about guilt than grace, more about our failings than Christ's forgiveness, is likely to have communion only rarely. A handful of times each year is the most frequently the congregation can cope with the grim discipline of this dour and rigorous self-scrutiny.

Those who think that God's saving power resides directly in the bread and wine will go to the opposite extreme. Just as a well-used car needs frequently to be filled with petrol, such Christians cannot get enough of communion, because it tops up their salvation. A new day is thought incomplete without the obligation of a new eucharist. Once again the New Testament provides a healthy corrective: the power of salvation is made available whenever human faith connects with divine grace. It is inward believing upon Christ, not the physical consumption of bread and wine that secures the gift of salvation.

Other Christians distort communion with a welter of rules and regulations. Irrespective of whether a church thinks of itself as 'liturgical' or 'non-liturgical', I have observed communions that are minutely, perhaps even obsessively codified. The poor congregation has little opportunity to meet with Christ during communion because they are too worried about making sure that they do the right thing at the right time. Communion can be the least welcoming Christian event for outsiders: it is not just the unchurched, but those from a different tradition, who can be quite thrown by the maze of correct behaviour that so often enmeshes what was originally a very simple meal.

Still other Christians continue to suffer from a reaction to medieval Catholicism. Some Protestant groupings were so disturbed by what they saw as an overstated emphasis on the Mass that the pendulum of church life kept swinging until it reached the opposite extreme. For such churches communion is treated as little more than an afterthought. The normal order of service is completed, and then a communion is tacked on at the end. For some there is a conscious desire to demonstrate what is seen as an ecclesiastical corrective: one Anglican vicar explained to his PCC that his approach was designed to demonstrate to other parishes the primacy of preaching. For others, there has been no conscious decision to marginalise communion: it is just the way things have 'always been done' in their church.

While some historic Protestant denominations have been tempted to tack communion onto their worship as a self-contained afterthought at the margins of their church life and spirituality, I have detected in some new churches a different kind of marginalisation. The breaking of bread can become so informal – no doubt in reaction against the rampant rules and regulations of the opposite excess – that it becomes casual, with little sense of the awesomeness of a transcendent God, or of the holy mystery that is intrinsic to this sacred meal. Blink and you will miss it – their communion is over in an instant, with no more sense of awe than is given to the coffee and biscuits provided after the service.

Because communion can become distorted in so many different ways, and because the pattern in many churches is repeated more or less on automatic pilot, with little sense of freshness, creativity or self-criticism, it is important to get back to our roots. Reflection upon the Scriptures will certainly not produce one 'right way' of 'doing communion'. But it should provide us with many creative insights, from which the distinctive style of our own tradition, ancient or modern, and also our own personal involvement and responsiveness to the meal of Jesus, can draw fresh ideas and inspiration.

To return to the feeling of unworthiness, we have recognised that it may be provoked by unhelpful emphases and less than adequate interpretations of the significance of communion. But in casting aside inappropriate, man-made feelings of unworthiness, we should be careful not to lose sight of the real thing. Christians who take their commitment seriously will necessarily remain aware of their own failings. It was in his mature years that Augustine declared that he realised the greatest problem in his Christian life was his own character. Dependence upon Christ for our salvation is not something we grow out of with the passing of years, unless we are lapsing into half-heartedness or complacency. The more we seek to live for Christ, the more we discover just how deeply ingrained and resilient in every one of us is the sinful nature.

Unworthiness is a perspective upon ourselves which is absolutely intrinsic to communion. Those who feel they do not deserve to eat and drink can take part with grateful hearts. As for the heirs of the Pharisees, who come to communion with a smug sense of spiritual superiority, confident that God must be as pleased with their lives as they are with themselves, communion has no benefit for them. This meal is reserved for the undeserving. It is for unworthy sinners only.

Prayer response

Give thanks that communion is a meal for the unworthy and that faith in Christ is the sole basis of participation.

2

A meal of remembrance – Christ has died

The Lord's Supper is a meal with a history. When Paul wrote to the Corinthians, he reminded them of Jesus' words of institution which he had already passed on to them, having received them 'from the Lord' (1 Cor. 11:23). The unchanging essence of the gospel as it is passed from generation to generation is a frequent Pauline theme. Timothy, for example, is instructed not only to guard the good deposit (2 Tim. 1:13–14), but also to entrust it to faithful teachers who can pass it in turn to the next generation (2 Tim. 2:2).

In the case of communion, Paul is clearly concerned to retain the purity and focus of words that go back to Jesus, so that in the breaking of bread there is a direct, verbal connection with the Jesus of history. In Jesus' words there is great emphasis upon 'remembrance of me', a phrase used of both the bread and the cup (1 Cor. 11:24, 25). Paul spells out the central implication of this remembrance when he explains that whenever we eat this bread and drink this cup we 'proclaim the Lord's death until he comes' (1 Cor. 11:26). This meal is therefore not simply Christocentric – a broad focus upon remembrance of Jesus – but specifically crucicentric – it is indeed the great Easter sacrifice for all humankind that we recall in the breaking of bread.

For British people, the only common usage of the word 'remembrance' is in the context of Remembrance Sunday. The dead are remembered with dignity and respect, in a manner that is formal and even sombre. Although the moment of ceremony is likely to contain thanks to God that the war dead gave their lives as a sacrifice for the sake of the freedom we continue to enjoy, the emphasis is not upon the benefits secured for us but the immense cost of so much loss of life. This familiar usage is therefore misleading when it comes to remembrance of Christ, setting a tone that is too heavy, regretful, even sorrowful. Indisputably, his death came with great personal suffering, and just as surely it was our sin that set him upon a Roman gibbet. But with the sorrow there must always be gratefulness and joy. For we remember neither a tragic accident, nor a premature death, nor the abortion of hope. Good Friday cannot be severed from Easter Sunday. The pain of the cross leads with sudden alacrity to the joy of the resurrection. Our remembrance is not merely of a life sacrificed for the sake of atonement, but also of an empty cross and tomb. Not only has Christ died, but, with overwhelming historical evidence that anyone can examine, he has been uniquely and indisputably raised from the dead. Our remembrance is of no dead hero, but of the One whose life proved inextinguishable.

Just as many restaurants today provide a plate of bread before any other food arrives, the Jews traditionally began meals by breaking bread and giving thanks to God. This normal Jewish custom was overlaid for the first Christians by the way Jesus broke bread at key moments in his ministry: before the 5,000 were fed (Luke 9:16); at the Last Supper (Luke 22:19); and in the house of the two disciples who had not recognised him upon the Emmaus road (Luke 24:35). In a four-step sequence, believers in every century have recalled the custom of Jesus: taking bread, giving thanks, breaking bread and eating it.

In addition to this background of the general Jewish custom, Jesus drew quite explicitly upon the Passover when he gave his followers their new memorial meal. In elaborate detail, the Passover meal recalled the wretchedness of slavery in Egypt, the miraculous liberation in which the sacrificial lamb played a pivotal role, and the subsequent journey to the land of promise. For the Jews, this meal celebrated the defining moment in their history, when God covenanted himself to the Jewish nation and demonstrated his readiness to be their deliverer. Their national identity had been constituted by the decisive experiences of the Exodus generation. Their hope in later days of difficulty, whether personal or national, was sustained by looking back in confidence at the God who had been demonstrably on their side. In the meal of remembrance, the rising generation was instructed in the most decisive and redemptive moment of Jewish history and the saving acts of the living God.

For Jesus' disciples, the breaking of bread becomes a new Passover, a celebration of God's new saving initiative in which Jesus himself is recognised as the 'lamb of God who takes away the sins of the world' (John 1:29). While Jesus speaks of the bread as 'my body' which is simply 'for you', the cup is 'the new covenant in my blood'. Several Old Testament prophets had foretold the provision of a new covenant that would accomplish inner change in the people of God. Jesus takes this existing Jewish hope and directly connects it with his impending death. Just as the Passover meal celebrated liberation from Egyptian slavery thanks to the mighty hand of God, Jesus gives his Church a meal for the new covenant, celebrating the means by which God would secure for us an even more decisive liberation from bondage to sin. The Jews were destined to face several periods of subservience to the later empires of the Middle East, and would fervently pray for a new saving initiative by the God of their forefathers. In Christ, however, the price of atonement is paid once for all. His is the redemptive act with no possibility of obsolescence; no additional sacrifice will ever need to be made.

Personal reflection

Pause to consider the amazing sacrifice of the first Easter, in order that God might offer rescue and reconciliation to his enemies.

3

An everyday meal

When we explored the meaning of 'daily bread' in Chapter III, we saw that Jesus extracted from the fairly elaborate menu of the Passover meal the two elements that were the most simple. In warm countries where the water is unsafe, wine is naturally the standard drink until Coca-Cola arrives in large quantities – apparently not even France is immune to its allure any longer, and the fashionable young are now claiming to prefer it to the outmoded pleasures of *vin rouge et blanc*. Everyone needs to stock up on carbohydrate, and while some depend on potatoes or pasta, rice or noodles, bread was the food to be found on every Middle Eastern table in the time of Jesus. While the kind of loaf might vary enormously from the tables of the rich to those of the poor, everyone could expect access to some kind of bread. The universal meal of discipleship is therefore a meal of remarkable simplicity, maximising its accessibility irrespective of our income, and no one should have reason to panic, faced with such a simple meal, about how to eat it 'properly'.

The early Christians not only celebrated the Lord's Supper, they also enjoyed love feasts. Just as Jesus' life was characterised by frequent meals with both friends and strangers, they recognised that there is something about sharing food that strengthens the bonds of fellowship among believers. John Chrysostom, one of the most golden-tongued preachers of the early centuries, described the way that churches would celebrate communion during their main meeting and then stay together for a fellowship banquet, 'the rich bringing their provisions with them and the poor and destitute being invited, and all feasting in common' (from Homily 27 on 1 Corinthians).

Sometimes it becomes difficult in the early Christian writings to discern where a Lord's Supper ends and a love feast begins, since the breaking of bread with thanksgiving and also a glass of wine were enjoyed at both events. In later generations, the love feast degenerated into over-indulgence and so church leaders pressed for it to be abandoned. But we can still trace in the early years both an innocent delight in enjoying meals together as the family of God, and also a fascinating blurring of the line between these two ways in which they broke bread.

For most Christians today, the Lord's Supper has only the slightest resemblance to a normal meal. It may be far more than merely symbolic in its meaning, but the tiny quantity of food and drink consumed makes it a strictly symbolic event, a ritualised meal like no other. The language and symbolism of the New Testament invites us to think again. When Paul was sailing towards Rome, he urged the sailors to take some food, after fourteen storm-tossed days when there had been no opportunity to eat. Luke describes the way that Paul then took bread, gave thanks to God, broke it and began to eat, which helped the others to relax and eat their fill. Since Paul's actions follow the customary sequence of the Lord's Supper, much theological ink has been spilt on whether Paul is sharing a eucharistic meal with unbelievers. But that misses the point entirely. Paul's actions can be understood at three levels: he is being practical, encouraging the starving men to eat and demonstrating thankfulness to the God who is the giver and preserver of our lives; he is being evangelistic, building points of contact with the gospel in this pre-eucharistic public breaking of bread; and he would also seem to be eating his own portion of bread with an added dimension of eucharistic significance.

Paul's actions indicate another level in the meaning of Jesus' words, when he spoke of us remembering him as often as we consume this simple meal. For the believer, every bite of bread and every sip of wine can become a moment of remembrance. The pivotal power of the cross of Christ breaks through into the ordinariness of daily living. It is not just that we are continually brought to remembrance of Christ's death. The ordinary is touched by the transcendent: we encounter God not exclusively in the religious sphere of Sunday worship, but even in the most trivial crumbs of daily living.

Unexceptional meals, without any conscious or obvious religious element or intent, begin to be seen from a new perspective, saturated with a hidden, yet profound depth of spiritual significance. A simple lunch just as much as an expensive restaurant meal can be kissed with heaven's presence. In Christ, the most apparently insignificant or 'secular' moments of our daily lives become transfigured by the sacred. Like the sun quickening the earth as the dawn heralds a new day, the presence of Christ rises upon our hearts, not just in church but in the sacrament of the ordinary. Just as the human race has never lost the thrill and wonder of greeting a new dawn, as we acknowledge the destiny-shaping decisiveness of the Saviour's death and resurrection, and his present availability by the Holy Spirit, the gracious presence of the living God rises again in our hearts and warms us with the radiant love of heaven. As often as we eat and drink, we can learn to do so in remembrance of him.

Personal reflection

How can you bring increased God-awareness into your everyday world?

4

A feast of love – Christ is risen

This wonderful meal of remembrance connects every generation of believers with the words and events of the first Easter. But that is not the sum of its power. The second great tense of this meal is present – Christ has not only been raised, as an event on the pages of human history, but he *is* raised, so that his Lordship is the foundational reality not merely of the church, but of the entire cosmos.

In the great hymn of Colossians 1 (vv. 15–20), Christ has a threefold relationship with the Church. He is its source, in the decisive saving events of the first Easter. He is its head, the only one with a rightful claim to be Lord of the Church. And he is its sustainer, keeping the Church together and working always to keep the Church on track with his unchanging purposes of reconciliation and love.

This glorious trio of truths is only half the story. He is also the source of creation, for it was by the pre-existent Son that all created things were brought into being at the dawn of the cosmos – in Christ's humanity his life quickened in Mary's womb at a specific moment in time, but in his divinity, the Word was with God and was God at the very beginning, before time began (John 1:1–2). He is the head of the cosmos, for all was created for him and therefore remains ultimately accountable to him. And he is the sustainer of the cosmos: far from an impulsive inventor who might turn aside once the novelty has worn off, he stays involved, keeping all things together, sustaining the gift of life in all its beauty, order, variety and vitality. J. B. Phillips once wrote a book called *Your God Is Too Small.* This glorious hymn of the cosmic Christ could be entitled, *Your Christ Is Too Small.* There is no part of life which cannot be suffused with new delight in the radiant presence of the Son: he is directly concerned with every aspect and every possibility of human existence, in the power of eternal love.

Because Christ has been raised as Lord, he is reigning for us over the entire cosmos. Paul adds the insight that he is interceding for us (Rom. 8:34) – constantly seeking the very best for his beloved, with a far better perspective upon our needs and potential than we could ever have. Risen and reigning, by the Holy Spirit Christ makes himself available to us. The Jesus of history is the Christ of today, encountering us inwardly with his holy love. At the time of the Wesleys and Whitefield, a wonderfully suggestive phrase was used to express this availability of the risen Lord, when they emphasised the need not merely to give mental assent to the gospel, but to know the 'felt Christ' in the innermost depths of our being.

Available at all times and in all places by his Spirit, the risen Christ is specially available in the communion encounter. Probably quoting words that were often used during the Lord's Supper in the first Christian generation, Paul described this encounter as a 'participation in Christ'.

> *Is not the cup of thanksgiving for which we give thanks a participation in the blood of Christ? And is not the bread that we break a participation in the body of Christ?*
>
> 1 Corinthians 10:16

In Christian experience, this participation is a living reality. Even the most cursory, marginalised, abrupt or casual communion service can be suffused with the risen presence that warms us within and quickens our spirit.

At the time of the Reformation, a great deal of theological reflection attempted to explore the precise way in which the risen Christ meets us in communion. Medieval Catholicism had developed the doctrine of transubstantiation, in which the bread and wine, while retaining the visual characteristics of ordinary food and drink, change their substance under the priestly prayer of consecration, so that they are actually transformed, materially, into the body and blood of Christ. This teaching depended on a pre-scientific understanding of the nature of matter, assuming that such a transformation of inner substance while retaining the original outward appearance was a physical possibility. A theory that has become obsolete was used to attempt to explain the participation in Christ that has continued to be a privilege of Christian experience in every generation. The medieval teaching had two consequences: first, if the literal body and blood are present, the sacrifice of Christ is presented anew to God – for the reformers, this seemed to trespass on the unique and decisive, once-for-all efficacy of the cross, to which no further, supplementary sacrifice need ever be added; second, if the literal body and blood are present, the sacrament should either be entirely consumed, for fear of its falling into the wrong hands, or it should be stored safely and venerated, worthy of devotion as the crucified Saviour's body and blood.

In reaction against this over-elaborate theory, which ran the risk of distracting people from the decisive historical events of the cross and resurrection, Zwingli developed a minimalist approach to the meaning of the Lord's Supper. Drawing on Latin usage of the word 'sacrament', he understood the sacrament of communion as a kind of oath of allegiance to Christ, a renewal of our covenant commitment in devotion and surrender. The weakness of this approach is that the word 'sacrament' is never used in the New Testament, so to define a Christian practice that began among Aramaic- and Greek-speaking people by means of the literal usage of a word in the Latin language requires a decidedly tortuous logic. For Zwingli, the Lord's Supper was a mere memorial – a recollection of the cross, devoid of present-day encounter. As so often in the Christian Church, in reaction against one over-statement, Zwingli lurched to the opposite extreme, stripping communion of the present-day dimension of encounter and participation in the presence of the risen Christ. Sadly there are still some free-church circles today who hold to this truncated theory, restricting their understanding of communion to the past tense alone.

Calvin and Luther both attempted to discover a middle path, preserving the uniqueness of the cross of Christ while giving due appreciation to the present-day reality of living encounter. Luther developed a theory of the 'real presence' – something palpable happens at the breaking of bread, that allows a depth of encounter. Luther's account of Christian experience has more lasting value than his attempted explanation, which still leaned upon outmoded medieval concepts of matter and substance that are themselves neither found within nor required by the biblical data. Calvin's middle path was less speculative and therefore more useful and lasting. While the physical constituents of bread and wine remain unchanged, he argued, there can be a simultaneous feeding upon Christ, by faith in our hearts. It is not that Christ's actual body is chewed in our mouths, which some have found an unnecessarily literal and even distasteful prospect. But the Holy Spirit mediates a simultaneous presence of Christ, who meets with us spiritually even *as* we eat, rather than physically *in* the food and drink we consume.

Christ's presence is real, but spiritual not physical. His presence is mediated not by the prayer of a priest, so that every fragment of bread is transubstantiated regardless of whether those who eat it have personal faith, which means a scrupulous avoidance of leaving any crumbs that mice or rats might consume. Rather, his presence is mediated by the Holy Spirit, so that participation in Christ is an extra dimension to the feast which requires the presence of personal, saving faith in the Christian communicant. We do not consume Christ automatically, irrespective of our own attitude towards him, but we feed on him in our hearts, nourished spiritually even as the bread and wine nourish us physically, as we draw near to him by faith and in dependence upon the Holy Spirit.

There is no need for us to embrace the anachronistic speculation of medieval Catholicism in order to explain our experiences of encounter with Christ in communion. Nor do we need to adopt the reductionist reaction of the more extreme reformers, restricting communion to the past tense alone. The Christ who promised that he would come to us by the Spirit, whom he would send as another Counsellor, visits his beloved in many different ways. But perhaps the most universal, the most frequent, is the participatory encounter of communion. Like the early disciples on the Emmaus road, who suddenly recognised the Master in the breaking of bread, we take the simplest of food and suddenly the risen Christ has dawned again in our hearts. And in his coming is abundant thankfulness and fullness of joy.

Personal reflection

When you take communion, do you embrace an experience of present encounter with Christ, or has it become a rather empty act of comformity, with little freshness, immediacy or spiritual vitality?

5

A meal together

Jesus was extremely keen on sharing meals with both friends and strangers. We read of many meals with his closest disciples, but also with people he met on his travels – keen enquirers, a Pharisee, and even a notoriously corrupt tax collector. Theologians have coined a rather quaint and archaic phrase to describe this willingness to share a meal – 'table fellowship'. The term hardly does justice to the warm-heartedness of Jesus. He was a people person, who loved company. The meal that he gave his followers is not designed to be a hole-in-the-corner, private event, best consumed by individuals on their own: there is no place in the Christian faith for a 'pot-noodle spirituality' in which individualistic believers resolutely isolate themselves from the rest of the Church. There are no lone-wolf disciples in the New Testament: leadership is in teams, missionary work is in teams, and the local church is called to function as God's new family. Those who are adopted by Father God must learn to love their fellow believers as brothers and sisters in Christ.

The fullest meaning of the Lord's Supper can only be expressed when a whole church eats and drinks together. This meal embodies the same priorities as the Lord's Prayer: just as Jesus instructed his followers to pray in the plural – '*Our* Father' – he provided a meal for his followers to eat together. Some of the early Church fathers suggested that churches should not offer communion more than once a week, in order to ensure that no misguided Christians would attempt to restrict the breaking of bread to their social set or exclusive circle of friends. This meal was seen as the cement of Church unity. Those who were sick were taken a portion of the bread and wine from the public communion, ensuring that they were not left out of this inclusive Christian privilege.

When Paul wrote 1 Corinthians, the church had fallen into a disgraceful abuse of communion: some were ravenous when they arrived and grabbed as much bread as they could, while others went without; they even abused the wine so that some became drunk while others were still hungry (1 Cor. 11:21). Paul was disgusted by this selfish disregard for one another and such an appalling irreverence for the communion feast. He therefore warned the Corinthians that God's judgment was upon them for their careless abuse of the sacred meal.

Paul provided two practical guidelines for the meal and an underlying principle. The practicalities were that believers should eat something before they left home, so that no one arrived at the meeting desperate for food; and secondly that they should wait for one another, which does not mean they should consume communion in the style of a synchronised swimming team, but simply that they should make sure that everyone was ready to take part together and no one missed out. The underlying principle was that they needed to recognise the 'body of the Lord' as they ate and drank (1 Cor. 11:29). From the context, this statement seems to have a double significance. First, they should be eating 'in a worthy manner', in other words with appropriate reverence, because otherwise they would be sinning against the Lord's body and blood. That is, they must take communion with due regard to Christ himself. Second, they must eat and drink with due regard for one another – a gluttonous and selfish pigging out is the chief offence for which Paul upbraids them, and the very next theme to which Paul turns is the Church as the body of Christ. In other words, they must recognise and express love towards the entire body of Christian believers, even as they eat and drink.

Paul's sharp rebuke of the Corinthians means there can be no excuse for any Christian taking communion and within minutes returning to wallow in the mire of complaints, gossip, judgmentalism and negativity. The lips that are blessed by the meal that Jesus provided should only be used to speak a blessing upon others. Our carping betrays us, demonstrating that we have failed to discern the body, with the result that we forfeit the presence of Jesus by his Spirit.

I have been present at communions which have been so cold and formal that everyone appears to be taking part from within a hermetically sealed cubicle. It is not that people have anything against each other, but the Lord's Supper has been reduced to an individualised, privatised, isolationist ritual. Because of an absolute avoidance of any kind of contact with other communicants – by words, by touch, or even by eye contact – we might as well be taking communion in the privacy of our own home. The togetherness of this meal can be strengthened by serving one another. Whether this is done by a team of servers or by serving the person next to you, two small steps make an enormous difference. First, the personal touch is enormously magnified simply by using the first name of those being served. Second, people need to be reassured that it is perfectly acceptable to use their normal speaking voice: there are still too many churches where people feel obliged to sink into an inaudible mutter once the distribution of communion has begun.

Sharing the peace is meant to reinforce our sense of belonging. For some Christians, the peace is a wonderful moment, and they look forward to the invitation to greet others with eager anticipation. For those with a more reserved temperament, the anticipation of this moment is filled with creeping anxiety: with grim determination they steel themselves for their most awkward moment in Christian worship. It has always seemed to me that the benefits of warmly greeting one another should be seen to outweigh the difficulty such a moment provokes for some. But the peace needs to be handled sensitively, giving the shy sufficient permission to be themselves, not feeling that they must somehow instantaneously metamorphose into bear-hugging, larger-than-life extroverts. Little is achieved if the peace degenerates into a stilted formality, with no more warmth than shaking a stranger's hand. A greeting within a service needs to be a fleeting expression of a deep-seated commitment to one another – the kind of brotherliness and sisterliness that Luke described when he said the first believers 'devoted themselves to the fellowship . . . and ate together with glad and sincere hearts' (Acts 2:42, 46).

There is much debate over whether young children are entitled to share in communion. Some argue that the traditional Anglican and Catholic pattern should be maintained, so that becoming a communicant must always be preceded by the twin rites of baptism and confirmation. Some argue that the sacrament of entry to full church membership is believers' baptism, so that the Lord's Supper should be reserved for those who are both believers and baptised. Others argue that communion only has meaning in the context of saving faith, and so the decisive factor is personal confession of faith, irrespective of the baptismal practices of different churches. Still others observe that while baptism is designed to be unrepeatable, there can be no limit on the number of times we can take communion, therefore those journeying towards faith may find it helpful to begin to take communion before they are ready to take the plunge in baptism.

While children need to grow into personal faith, and cannot in adulthood rely on the birthright of their parents' discipleship, in childhood they are under the provisional covering of their parents' faith. This is what Paul seems to be arguing, when he states that where one half of a couple is not a Christian, their children are 'holy' through the faith of the believing parent (1 Cor. 7:14). Paul makes no reference here to infant baptism, but the implications for communion need to be explored whether our church concludes that such a practice is a logical consequence or an illogical distraction from the force of his argument. For me, the connection with Passover is significant, since that was a covenant meal for the whole family. The pattern I have followed for many years is not to distribute the elements to young children, but rather to explain to their parents that they have the right of discretion. If they prefer, they may wish to have hands laid on their children for a prayer of blessing. But others will want to break off some of their bread and share it with their children. I know of few moments more moving in the Christian faith than to see entire families sharing in the feast of Christ in this simple and beautiful way, with the nuclear family set within the inclusive family of the people of God, where young and old, single and married, rich and poor, successful and struggling, all eat together and recognise one another as brothers and sisters within God's new family of love.

Personal reflection

How can the New Testament values of togetherness and belonging find their fullest expression in your local church?

6

A feast of eternity – Christ will come again

This is a meal with a future. Just as the Lord's Prayer connects the present with the past and future coming of the kingdom of God, the Lord's Supper connects us with both the first Easter and the promised Great Return. Jesus makes the sense of anticipation emphatic by stressing that he will not consume this meal again 'until the kingdom of God comes' (Luke 22:18). The distinctive meal of the Christian Church therefore sets our present circumstances firmly between the two most decisive events of human history: the Christ of the cross and the final judgment provide a gilt-edged hope. The bread and the wine are the enduring symbols of what he has already accomplished and the enduring pledge that he will complete what he has begun.

This promise of a wondrous future comes to us not as a charter for timetables and idle speculation, but to set our daily concerns in the perspective of eternity. This life is but a prelude and preparation for the prospect of heaven. There is no need for the Christian to get sucked into living for today as an end in itself. Today is a gift to be enjoyed to the full, but eternity is an incomparably more glorious prospect to which we look forward with great expectancy.

Communion can be seen as soul medicine. Not that there are literal healing properties in the bread and wine. But as we eat and drink in thankfulness and expectancy, this meal adjusts our perspective on life. It is a meal of peace, in which the gracious and saving accomplishments of Christ can drain away all fears and anxieties.

The ultimate meal to which Jesus invites us to look forward is very different from every present-day experience of communion, irrespective of our denomination or stream. Until that time, the note of longing will always be present, as we eagerly desire the return of Christ and the end of history. At his return, the meal will be nothing less than the wedding banquet of the Lamb. Hope will give way to consummation, undeservedness to a celebration of the triumph of grace, in the biggest party ever given for the human race.

In an age of constantly accelerating change, TV programmes that predict the future quickly look ridiculous. Every time we buy sophisticated electronic appliances, within months a new model makes ours look old fashioned. But Jesus' promised return has no sell-by date, no built-in obsolescence. His word is utterly reliable, and so our security in him is rock solid. Every breaking of bread inks over our sure and certain future hope. The Lamb of God will surely return and we will delight in his feast of victory when he welcomes us into the fullness of his kingdom.

Before the arrival of that final, glorious day, death ushers us into eternity. The most moving communions I have ever taken have been with those on the brink of death. I think of Sonya, a Swedish woman who knew she would never see the country of her birth again. The hospice had sent her home to die, tubes linking her to a machine that pumped regular doses of painkillers into her veins. There are times when communion and prayers for healing sit well together. It is a delight to anoint with oil those who are seeking the healing mercy of their risen Lord. But communion is also a fitting meal in the face of death. The same Jesus restores us to health and helps us prepare to die.

Sonya could only speak slowly through the numbing blur of her drugs. But she knew that she wanted one more breaking of bread. As we ate and drank together, the meal of Jesus was soul medicine for us both, the young minister with a lifetime stretching ahead of him, and the dying woman, the skin of her face stretched like paper over protruding cheekbones, her body fat consumed by the trauma of terminal illness. I was strengthened for life by the body and blood. Sonya was strengthened for death. She tired quickly, and after we had shared the simple meal of Jesus she was soon asleep. This world would see no more breaking of bread for Sonya. The next time she ate and drank she would see Jesus face to face, filled with eternal vitality and resurrection joy at the wedding banquet of the Lamb. His indeed is the kingdom, the power and the glory, for ever and ever. Amen.

Prayer response

Pray that, in your last days, you will know the Lord's Supper and the Lord's Prayer ushering you into God's eternal kingdom.

7

Bible Meditation

LEVITICUS 16:20–6

The scapegoat was a remarkable annual symbol of divine forgiveness in ancient Israel. It must have been a supercharged moment of drama in the nation's religious life when a live goat was brought before Aaron. With the laying-on of hands, there was a symbolic transfer of sin from the people to the goat. Aaron's prayer was no jingoistic expression of patriotic fervour, for this was no celebration of national triumphs. Instead Aaron freely confessed the wickedness and rebellion of the nation. No observer of the ceremony would have been in any doubt that Israel's standing before God was due to God's patience and covenant mercy rather than the merit of the nation's behaviour.

The person responsible for the goat would then lead it into the desert, only abandoning it when there was no prospect that it would find its way back among the people. Left alone, the goat would wander into a remote and solitary place, from which neither it, nor the sins which had been laid symbolically upon its head, would return.

The ceremony must have made an unforgettable impact. Crucial moral principles of guilt and forgiveness were vividly enacted before the people's eyes. They were taught the seriousness of sin before a holy God, the universality of sin as the guilt of all Israel was acknowledged, and the possibility of free and full forgiveness with the transfer of sin and guilt to the scapegoat.

For the Christian, this remarkable ancient ceremony is a dramatic preparation for the atoning sacrifice of Christ. At the cross he has become our scapegoat, and so in every remembrance of his death we take full account of the enormity of human sin and the extravagance of the saving love of God. Here is no symbolic scapegoat, a domesticated animal unwittingly recruited for the festival of atonement. Instead, it is the Son of God who voluntarily surrenders his life not merely for his closest friends, which would have taken courage and self-sacrifice enough, but even for the most hardened enemies of God.

In every recollection of the cross, and above all in the Lord's Supper, we celebrate and marvel at the saving power of Christ's atoning death. In his crucifixion, burial and resurrection are found the eradication of sin and the promise of a divine mercy and grace that are inextinguishable. At times we may be moved to mourn the extremity of suffering to which Christ was taken by our sin. But our sorrow can always be tempered by grateful thanks, for his death and resurrection demonstrate the triumph of the Father's saving love. The Lamb who was slain has begun his reign, and to him be all praise for ever and ever! Amen.

DEVOTIONAL POEMS

That day of wrath, that dreadful day,
When heaven and earth shall pass away,
What power shall be the sinner's stay?
How shall he meet that dreadful day?

When, shrivelling like a parched scroll,
The flaming heavens together roll;
When louder yet, and yet more dread,
Swells the high trump that wakes the dead;

Oh! On that day, that wrathful day,
When man to judgment wakes from clay,
Be THOU the trembling sinner's stay,
Though heaven and earth shall pass away!

Sir Walter Scott, 1771–1832

PEACE

My soul, there is a country
Far beyond the stars,
Where stands a winged sentry
All skilful in the wars:
There above noise and danger
Sweet peace sits crown'd with smiles,
And one born in a manger
Commands the beauteous files.
He is thy gracious friend,
And (O my soul awake!)
Did in pure love descend
To die here for thy sake,
If thou canst get but thither,
There grows the flower of peace,
The Rose that cannot wither,
Thy fortress and thy ease;
Leave then thy foolish ranges;
For none can thee secure,
But one, who never changes,
Thy God, thy life, thy cure.

Henry Vaughan, 1621–95

In the hour of my distress,
When temptations me oppress,
And when I my sins confess,
Sweet Spirit, comfort me!

When I lie within my bed,
Sick in heart and sick in head,
And with doubts discomforted,
Sweet Spirit, comfort me!

When the house doth sigh and weep,
And the world is drowned in sleep,
Yet mine eyes the watch do keep,
Sweet Spirit, comfort me!

When, God knows, I'm tossed about,
Either with despair, or doubt;
Yet before the glass be out,
Sweet Spirit, comfort me!

When the judgment is revealed,
And that opened which was sealed,
When to thee I have appealed,
Sweet Spirit, comfort me!

Robert Herrick, 1591–1674

Never weather-beaten sail more willing bent to shore,
Never tired pilgrim's limbs affected slumber more,
Than my weary sprite now longs to fly out of my troubled breast,
O come quickly, sweetest Lord, and take my soul to rest!

Ever blooming are the joys of heaven's highest paradise,
Cold age deafs not there our ears nor vapour dims our eyes:
Glory there the sun outshines; whose beams the blessed only see,
O come quickly, glorious Lord, and raise my sprite to Thee!

Thomas Campion, 1567–1620

This is my play's last scene, here heavens appoint
My pilgrimage's last mile; and my race
Idly, yet quickly run, hath this last pace,
My span's last inch, my minute's latest point,
And gluttonous death, will instantly unjoint
My body and soul, and I shall sleep a space,
But my ever-waking part shall see that face,
Whose fear already shakes my every joint:
Then, as my soul, to heaven her first seat, takes flight,
And earth born body, in the earth shall dwell,
So, fall my sins, that all may have their right,
To where they are bred, and would press me, to hell.
Impute me righteous, thus purg'd of evil,
For thus I leave the world, the flesh, the devil.

John Donne

Further Reading

Augustine	*Confessions*
Benedict	*The Rule of St Benedict*
Bernard of Clairvaux	*On the Love of God*
David Brainerd (ed. J. Edwards)	*The Life and Death of David Brainerd*
John Bunyan	*Pilgrim's Progress*
	Grace Abounding
Alan Ecclestone	*Yes to God*
Jonathan Edwards	*The Religious Affections*
Sarah Edwards	*Journal* (found within the memoir of Jonathan Edwards, *Complete Works*, vol. I)
Ruth Etchells (ed.)	*Praying with the English Poets*
Richard Foster	*Celebration of Discipline*
	Prayer
Marjory Foyle	*Honourably Wounded*
Francis of Assisi	*The Little Flowers of St Francis*
James Gordon	*Evangelical Spirituality*
O. Hallesby	*Prayer*
David Hanes (ed.)	*My Path of Prayer*
Walter Hilton	*The Stairway of Perfection*
James Houston	*The Transforming Friendship*

Joyce Huggett	*Listening to God*
	The Smile of Love
Basil Hume	*Searching for God*
John of the Cross	*The Dark Night of the Soul*
Julian of Norwich	*Revelations of Divine Love*
Thomas Kelly	*A Testament of Devotion*
Thomas à Kempis	*The Imitation of Christ*
William Law	*A Serious Call to a Devout and Holy Life*
Brother Lawrence	*The Practice of the Presence of God*
Ignatius Loyola	*The Spiritual Exercises*
Gordon Macdonald	*Ordering Your Private World*
	Restoring Your Spiritual Passion
Floyd McLung	*The Father Heart of God*
Nether Springs Community	*A Northumbrian Office*
John Newton	*Letters*
Henry Nouwen	*The Genessee Diary*
	Creative Ministry
	The Wounded Healer
J. I. Packer	*Knowing God*
Blaise Pascal	*Pensées*
Eugene Peterson	*A Long Obedience in the Same Direction*
Richard Rolle	*The Fire of Love*
J. C. Ryle	*Holiness*
Frances de Sales	*Introduction to the Devout Life*
Ray Simpson	*Exploring Celtic Spirituality*
John R. W. Stott	*The Message of the Sermon on the Mount*
Jeremy Taylor	*Holy Living*
Helmut Thielicke	*The Prayer that Spans the World*
Abbé de Tourville	*Letters of Spiritual Direction*
Simon Tugwell	*Ways of Imperfection*

Evelyn Underhill	*The Spiritual Life*
Charles Wesley	*Hymns* (one excellent selected edition is *A Flame of Love*, ed. T. Dudley-Smith
John Wesley	*Journals*
George Whitefield	*Journals*

ANONYMOUS WRITINGS AND COMPILATIONS

Cloud of Unknowing
The Lives and Sayings of the Desert Fathers
The Philokalia
Rule for a New Brother
Theologica Germanica

Hymn books have traditionally been understood to provide invaluable resources for personal prayer. Many Christians now find this need is met, at least in part, through worship tapes and CDs. But recordings do not readily encourage meditation upon the words of a song or hymn. I would therefore recommend *The Source*, edited by Graham Kendrick, as the most comprehensive and exceptional modern compilation of ancient and modern hymns and songs, that is sure to provide a goldmine of spiritual enrichment not only for public worship, but for personal praise and prayer.

WALKING WITH GOD

A companion volume to PRAYING WITH JESUS

Rob Warner

In a world of frenetic schedules, prayer can seem a non-productive luxury for which we cannot afford the time . . . and yet we long for a deeper sense of spiritual vitality and reality.

WALKING WITH GOD is a book for ordinary people with busy lives. Through the example of Christ and the witness of the great Christian writers, Rob Warner shows us how prayer can create the still centre of being in our lives and provide the fertile ground on which effective and creative living can be grown.

With the use of biblical meditation, devotional poems from great poets and prayers from spiritual leaders, this book inspires us afresh towards prayer and renewed spiritual growth. It will be helpful to individuals, for use during Lent or in daily readings, and for house groups who want to explore dimensions of prayer together.

0 340 71015 2